D1545073

DEVELOPMENT THEORY: CRITIQUES AND EXPLORATIONS

Also by A.H. Somjee

VOTING BEHAVIOUR IN AN INDIAN VILLAGE
POLITICAL THEORY OF JOHN DEWEY
DEMOCRACY AND POLITICAL CHANGE IN
  VILLAGE INDIA
DEMOCRATIC PROCESS IN A DEVELOPING
  SOCIETY
POLITICAL CAPACITY IN DEVELOPING SOCIETIES
POLITICAL SOCIETY IN DEVELOPING COUNTRIES
PARALLELS AND ACTUALS OF POLITICAL
  DEVELOPMENT
REACHING OUT TO THE POOR (*with Geeta Somjee*)

Development Theory: Critiques and Explorations

A.H. Somjee
Professor of Political Science
Simon Fraser University, Canada

St. Martin's Press   New York

First published in the United States of America in 1991

Printed in Hong Kong

ISBN 0–312–04886–6

Library of Congress Cataloging-in-Publication Data
Somjee, A.H.
    Development theory: critiques and explorations. / A.H. Somjee.
        p.   cm.
    Includes bibliographical references and index.
    ISBN 0–312–04886–6
    1. Economic development 2. Developing countries—Economic
    policy. I. Title
HD75.S65 1991
338.9'001—dc20   90–8552
                                                                   CIP

Dedicated to the memory of Professor N. C. Chatterji
who stimulated an interest in social and political theory in
a generation of students and made them aware of the work
to be done before it can claim to be universally valid

Contents

Preface

This book is about the deep inroads which the social sciences, with their specific approaches and theories, have made into development studies, thereby preventing the latter from addressing themselves to different and, in some cases, unique problems of their own. The social sciences and their corpus of theoretical knowledge are almost entirely rooted in the historical and social experiences of a few industrialised societies of the West. Development studies, on the other hand, are all about the problems of economic growth, political development and social change of developing societies which have come through historical and cultural experiences of a different kind. Moreover, the variety of backgrounds of different developing societies has also differently influenced their own development processes. However, the existing development studies, and their corpus of theoretical knowledge, which has largely come from the social sciences, show little or no sensitivity to the basic differences in development experiences of different societies. The net result of this is that we are often unable to pay sufficient attention to some of their crucial problems.

Moreover, the tendency of the social sciences to chop and slice the development process, so as to suit their own specialist requirements, has prevented scholars from addressing their theoretical efforts to the understanding of the complexity of the process in different societies, and then coming up with a nuanced analysis of the unique development experience of each. Whatever we have in scholarly literature on the development process is an assumed replication of what the industrialised societies of the West went through. In development studies, therefore, we need a fresh round of cognitive effort which can be focussed on the perceiving, knowing and conceptualising of the actual complexity of the development process in emerging societies.

The manner in which the social sciences have developed – as a result of the need to know more about the new problems of economy, society, and political institutions; by means of an adequate rationale for fresh intellectual subdivisions to study them independently of one another; then by a search for discrete variables and their relationships, including causal relationships, so that they qualify as 'science'; and, above all, by social scientists repeatedly asserting the intellectual self-sufficiency of the aspect of the social phenomena they were interested in – is increasingly being realised as unhelpful to development studies. This is because the demands of development studies run in the other direction. For unlike the social sciences, the demands of development studies are more in the direction of the inclusion of social, economic and political factors, in their mutually interactive relationships, which trigger off or stifle the development process itself. Development studies want to understand the complexity of such a process, across the disciplinary divide, come out with a nuanced analysis which is more meaningful to them, explore how external intervention can make a difference to such a process, and not barter away all this to be able to qualify – within the established intellectual traditions of the social sciences for rigour, abstraction and analysis – as a 'science'.

Such a divergence in approach, purpose, and intellectual standard between the two would not have mattered but for the fact that the social sciences began pre-empting large chunks of development studies for their own discipline-embedded approaches. The econo-mists carved out an area for themselves, from development studies, and began calling it economic growth; political scientists christened their haul political development; and the sociologists and anthropolo-gists started calling whatever they were interested in, social change. They then brought to bear the theoretical approaches and perspectives of their respective disciplines into the new territory into which they had extended themselves. Barring a few exceptions, as we shall see in this book, they rarely faced the intellectual challenge that was implicit in such an extension.

What we thus have, by way of development studies, is what the social scientists as practitioners of their own discipline have brought to bear on it. The peculiarities of their disciplinary approaches, theoretical limitations, and aversion to having anything to do with fellow social scientists interested in corresponding or even identical problems, continued even in their new field of endeavour.

But the social sciences' incursion into development studies brought to bear on the latter yet another limitation of their own. And that is, since the social sciences themselves were developed, by and large, to explain the historical and social experiences of a few industrialised societies of the West, the corpus of theoretical knowledge developed by them often has showed insensitivity to the different kinds of experiences which developing countries have gone through. Consequently, through the approaches of the social sciences, and more specifically by the unqualified use of their corpus of theoretical knowledge, we often miss out on some of the peculiar, and often crucial, problems of non-Western societies.

With our social science background we are preconditioned to looking at the parallels of Western historical and social developments in non-Western societies and, therefore, are likely to distort the actualities of those societies in our analysis of them.[1] Later on we shall have occasion to point out that while economic growth in Western societies may have attained its own independence from cultural and social forces, as Gunnar Myrdal has maintained,[2] that is not true of the non-Western societies. And to the extent to which we ignore such basic differences between them, we are likely to distort what we see, analyse or report.

Among the social sciences, particularly, economics has been the major role player in development studies. And so far as 'policies' for development are concerned, they are almost always based in the science of economics. But this new responsibility for economics has come at a time when of all the disciplines it has become the most inward looking. Such were the fears of the well-known development economist Albert Hirschman. In his words: "' . . . the discipline [of economics] became professionally more narrow at precisely the moment when the problem [of development] demanded broader, more political, and social insights".'[3] Simultaneously, the intellectual tradition of political economy, and the consideration of broader philosophical and moral issues with which the science of economics began in the eighteenth and nineteenth century, were relegated to the other disciplines. Since then its insular tendency has been further reinforced by the application of the independent intellectual machinery of mathematics, deductivistic reasoning, and a theoretical play on continuous model-building based on shortlived assumptions. There would have been much less reason to complain about all these intellectually respectable cognitive processes had they not been extended, in an unqualified manner, into the complex terrain of development, where approaches which are exclusively based on such intellectual tools appear extraneous, naïve, and even distortive of a phenomenon which is a complex intermesh of several forces. A number of top-flight development economists such as Myrdal, Schumpeter, Hoselitz, Hirschman, Amartya Sen and Paul Streeten, repeatedly came out with their scholarly critiques of such a drift but could do precious little to change the unqualified application of the approaches of economics to development studies.

The disciplines of political science, sociology and, particularly, anthropology, which were from their very inception much more used to recognising the interconnectedness of their specific areas with others, were more at home with the demands of development studies. But they too did not make any significant attempt at treating such demands as constituting a new challenge which called for a fresh round of cognitive effort.

In strict theoretical terms, therefore, whatever 'advances' were reported in development studies were, by and large, advances in different branches of the social sciences, with a limited degree of applicability to development studies proper.

The fact of the matter, then, is that the way in which the social sciences have been allowed to make incursions into development studies, without the needed additional effort to ensure their suitability, may be considered to be the greatest single factor preventing the possible emergence of development studies as a branch of knowledge struggling to be a discipline, with intellectual tools that are more suitable to its own peculiar problems.

One of the concerns of this book, therefore, is to critique the various social science-embedded approaches, and to explore the possibility of different approaches, taking into account the actualities of grassroots development experiences. There is much to be learnt from the past development experiences of developing societies themselves. They, in fact, have much more to teach us, at least at this stage, than our segmented, and Western development experience-based, social science theories.

The theoretical component of the social sciences, apart from their respective insistence on the 'purity' of their phenomena – economics unsullied by cultural factors, politics undisplaced from the crucial decision-making position, and sociology as encompassing the social whole towering well above other subsystems – is also given to a reductionist bias. Their theoretical component has thus maintained, repeatedly, its proclivity towards reducing the often irreducible and complex, to a few self-defined crucial factors, and from there to a few discrete variables. After that a correspondence between discrete variables and their analytical relationships, and the social reality, is taken for granted. In the unmistakable positivistic tendency of the natural sciences, the 'scientific' aspect of social science theory also assumes that the only way to get at the social reality is by means of identifying crucial variables, first, and then conceptually grasping analytical relationships between them, with or without empirical or historical research into the background of those variables.

Such a reductionist bias, rooted in social science theory, does not sit well with the complex world of development, with its own continuum of forces of history, tradition and culture, and all these deeply enmeshed in efforts at economic growth, political development, and social change. And the more you try to cut off into neat variables, what Schumpeter called 'the social whole', to suit the specialist requirement of your branch of the social sciences, the more abstracted and unreal it becomes, and so does your understanding of it. To be precise, the demands of development studies run counter to what the practitioners of the social sciences have got used to regarding as 'scientific'.

This then brings us to the controversial, and, in recent years, methodologically forbidden, approach of inductive knowledge. The constraint on inductive knowledge – arising out of a logical case against the very possibility of such knowledge – in our context would mean that we cannot learn from past development experiences nor can we make them a possible source of theory construction along with our initial hunches and hypotheses.

A generation of field research scholars in the social sciences has methodologically subscribed to a schizophrenic position of collecting empirical data, beyond their initial hunches and hypotheses, and also holding fast to Karl Popper's position of the impossibility of induction in human knowledge. Popper extracted, as it were, a promise from them never to embark on field research without a range of hunches and hypotheses. For Popper, once a hunch or an assertion or even a hypothesis breaks down in the conduct of research, you come back to construct another, and then resume your research. The wrecked hypothesis has no value. For Karl Popper there is no room for the messy meandering conduct of actual research, where one's initial hunches, and laboriously constructed hypotheses break down in the first few days or even within moments of field research, and around the wreckage itself one collects a lot of data, which subsequently, and, alas, inductively, sustain reconstructed hypotheses. So in the conduct of actual social science field research, your progression is from: hypotheses to their wreckage, to collecting of data round the wreckage, hoping that the data will be useful some day, to trying out what such already collected data *can* sustain by way of different and unthought-of hypotheses.

The world of development experience is one such area where you get steered, or shipwrecked, into the connected situations by related forces that you had not envisaged had existed when you embarked on your research with your initial set of hypotheses. Round the wreckage of your hypotheses you get a sense of how various interconnections and interactions, which are an integral part of the development process, actually work. And, in your final research statement, it is your discovery, understanding, and analysis of development interconnections and interactions that you identify and communicate.

But to buy one's methodological peace, one remains a self-unconfessed inductionist in the conduct of one's actual research, on the one hand, and an induction-denying Popperian in one's professional posture, on the other. That indeed is a far cry from the neat world of theory where consistency, honesty in intellectual position, and truth are highly regarded. And yet one's excursions into the complex world of development experience have another story to tell. Hence a methodological schizophrenia.[4]

The deeper we go into development experience, beyond the enforced parallelism and induction-rejection approaches, the more we realise how much of a radical shift, from what we are methodologically trained for in our graduate schools, do we need to be able to respond adequately to the challenges of such experiences. For the intellectual challenge which development studies present us with is mind boggling, requiring an Archimedean shift in our perspectives, intellectual symbols, tools of knowledge, and what Max Weber called *verstehen* or the depth of understanding.[5] Edwin Ardener has referred to the problem of pre-empting intellectual symbols in favour of whichever region, situation, gender or problem received the initial attention.[6]

The economists prefer to have a single dimension approach, namely economic. This is an approach which they have picked up from the English Utilitarians in the eighteenth century at the very inception of their 'science', and even when they are analysing economic growth, where far too many interrelated factors are involved, or when they advise on development 'policy', where complex choices are to be made, neither of which can be fully dealt with by the self-imposed single dimensionality of economics. The well-known economist Joseph Schumpeter warned economists against treating economics as a complete universe. He wanted the students of economics to go back to the social contexts of economic facts. He even maintained that in any causal explanation, when all the factors identified are 'economic', then something has been left out. For him we can either begin or end our causal explanations with economic factors, but cannot do both.[7]

In economic growth the problem is not simply to formulate a specific development policy, and then find funds for its implementation, but also to gain a clear understanding of the social and cultural complexity of the target area, the individual and group dynamics or the lack thereof which caused the condition of underdevelopment in the first place, the basic economic factors involved, and a host of other related issues. The words 'economic growth' bring to mind a host of development co-ordinates, not all of which are confined to any particular social science discipline. The self-imposed purity of approach of the economists, while analysing the problems of economic growth, especially in developing countries, where, as Gunnar Myrdal pointed out, it has not become independent of cultural factors, is inadequate given the complexity of the issues involved.

The purists among the political scientists, too, have similar inadequacy in their approach to political development. In the growth of human political capacity to secure response and accountability from public officials, a range of non-political as well as political factors are involved. Moreover, the bulk of developing countries have been engaged in emulating Western legal and political institutions, practices and ideals, and the peculiar manner in which these operate, adapting themselves to different social and cultural contexts, cannot be explained in purely political terms.

Even within the different branches of the social sciences, which, as we noted earlier, have moved into the new field of development studies, there are critics of the way in which such a progression has occurred. We shall analyse their emphases, dissatisfactions, scholarly criticisms, and attempts at the reformulation of the respective approaches under the subtitles of development purists, interrelationists, and integrationists.

In our search for what all to look for in development studies, one of the most useful exercises is to examine the variety of development experiences in various broad regions, and the manner in which the various scholars from those regions have viewed their development problems. Those scholars, as we shall see, have seriously questioned the sensitivity and adequacy of the corpus of theoretical knowledge that was, first of all, developed to explain the social and historical problems of Western industrialised societies, and then, without many qualifications, extended to the study of non-Western societies.

Through their writings and critiques, they have made us aware of the need for a fresh round of cognitive effort before development theory can justify its claim to universal validity. What we so far have by way of such a theory is entirely based on the development experiences of a few industrialised societies of the West. And whatever such a theory cannot identify, or explain, does not become any less important to the regions in which it occurs.

In that connection we shall examine the broad social explanations of the development of the Western societies themselves. After that we shall take up the emphasis on international economic relationships put forward by scholars from Latin America to explain the peculiarities of the uneven development process in the two American continents. Finally, we shall take up the perspectives of some of the Asian scholars on the development process of their region, with its thick overlay of culture and traditional values influencing economic growth and political development.

An increased awareness of the variety of the development processes of different regions of the world will also make us conscious of the inadequacy of our theoretical knowledge in understanding them. It will demonstrate that so far we have been adamantly hanging on to the intellectual and theoretical capital generated, from eighteenth century onwards, largely to explain the development of industrialised societies, and that now we are extending it, without any additional effort, to societies which have come through a very different kind of social and historical experience.

In order to zero in on the deeply enmeshed forces – economic, social, cultural, political, and human – in the development process, we shall closely analyse the complexity of such a process, at the grassroots level, in one developing society, and identify the variety of human responses to development stimuli. This section will be based on my longitudinal field research in rural communities in western, eastern, and southern India, spread over nearly thirty years.

The variety of development initiatives launched by India, namely public, private, co-operative, and human self-rebuilding, in what may be regarded as one of the most complex societies in the world, will then give us a glimpse of the interrelations of the various factors involved in such initiatives, and the differentiated human responses to them. In all those development efforts one thing stands out unmistakably, and that is: in a situation of antecedent social inequality, which is far more complex and deeply rooted than the social scientists, so far, have a grip on, the human response to development stimuli is also different. A baffling illustration of this is that after nearly four decades of planned development, with 'socialist society' as her goal, India has earned the unenviable distinction of doubling the number of her people below the poverty line since independence.

Clearly, therefore, her policies based on pure, and largely imported, economic science, have proved to be disastrously inadequate. For this no economic advisor, indigenous or foreign, who was involved in her policy-making, can or should disown responsibility. Scapegoating apart, the greatest single mistake they made was in not understanding the complexity of the terrain where development efforts were targeted. Such complexities cannot be grasped through the exclusive perspectives of economics.

In that connection the present work takes up the problem of 'poverty'. There is much more to the poor in India than their economic deprivation. For since the dawn of Indian civilisation, right up to the present day, the poor in India have always been from the lower castes, untouchables, and tribals. Clearly, therefore, there must always have been *some* connection between one's economic condition and place in society. Moreover, much of India's notorious *karmic* rationale – of viewing one's present condition with reference to one's deeds in previous life – was directed, by and large, towards the lower strata in her caste system so that they, the lower castes and poor, might come to terms with what they had. Furthermore, Indian social and political movements have rarely touched her lower strata, thus leaving them with a crippled political capacity even when she emerged as a democratic society after independence. Finally, even during the period of planned development, when the poor have been specifically targeted for development, the bulk of them in rural communities have so deeply internalised a sense of marginality that they do not believe that those development efforts are for them. Consequently, we are not at all justified in viewing the poor, and their poverty, as a problem in 'pure' economics. It is indeed a many-sided problem, requiring a far more comprehensive effort than the economists have the sensitivity, intellectual tools, or, as Gunnar Myrdal felt, requisite approach for. And at stake here is not whether our academic model, and analysis, are 'correct', but the continued suffering of the world's largest pool of poor.

Intensive field research in various parts of India has shown that even when a few individuals within the traditional lower social strata have been able to improve their economic condition, their own social indignity and political ineffectiveness have continued. And so far as the social groups to which they belonged have been concerned, the economic improvements of a few individuals from among them have not brought about any change in their lives.[8]

If the economic deprivation of the poor is not their only problem, the question then is whether the continued social indignity, *karmic* rationale, implying that the poor get what they deserve, political incapacity, and a deeply internalised sense of marginality towards whatever is going on in the mainstream of society, have, together, done incalculable harm to the poor as human beings or not? Throughout India's great effort in building a classical civilisation, launching one of the boldest democratic experiments history has ever known, and making a success of it, and through her planned efforts at building agricultural, industrial, educational and infrastructural bases for her continued many-sided development, have not her poor continued to remain, for want of a better expression, a diminished people? After building one of the most uncaring traditional social organisations, the question is what would restore her poor to their full humanhood and potential?

For that purpose a section of this book is devoted to what I have called *ethnodevelopment*, which implies that over and above the vastly extended economic and educational opportunities for the poor, what will also be necessary is to involve the poor themselves in their own development. Their stunted human growth will not be restored if they are simply made the recipients of what the bureaucrats have to give to them by means of provisions of public policy. Their self-development has also to take place through their own involvement so that they may emerge, like any other citizen, as the demanders and takers of what is rightfully theirs.[9] Our understanding of these and related issues will then reveal complex reasons why there are differentiated human responses to uniform development stimulus.

But what interferes most in our efforts to know more about development experiences, is what I have called *the theory culture*, which we have allowed to develop in the social sciences. Justifiably or otherwise, we are used to questioning theory, often with the help of a rival theory. Along with that we are also used to abandoning a theory when it meets challenges from empirical evidence. But what we do not do, as stated earlier, is to build another theory based on such evidence. Such a theory culture, of indefinitely playing with rival theories, we have, arguably, acquired from the social sciences, and they, in turn, have acquired it from what they thought the prestigious and trend-setting natural sciences were doing. While all that theory making and breaking continues to be in a state of methodological uncertainty, which the social sciences with their academic interest can well afford, in development studies we cannot let go any kind of development experience with significance for our theory construction. While development studies can learn from what finally comes out of the interminable clash of speculative theories, and insights generated by it, they have to remain closer to their primary source, namely, the antecedent development experience itself. Such an emphasis can then be seen as a renewed preference for development empiricism in development studies and development theory.

To gain a wider perspective on development, no matter how very vague it may be initially, or incapable of precise definition, we need to have some exploratory notions of what development ought to consist of. We need to articulate more what such notions would imply without waiting for a universally acceptable definition of them to emerge. After all neither 'justice' nor 'freedom' have been conclusively defined, despite efforts in that direction since the dawn of human civilisation, and yet scholars have written exploratory treatises on them, and individuals and legislators have given expression to what they think these ought to consist of. We need to add a normative component to development studies so as to give a sense of direction to their highly specific undertakings. With all its shortcomings my notion of ethnodevelopment belongs to such a genre of thinking in development studies.

In development studies we need to go back, once again, to the theoretical drawing board for yet another round of cognitive effort. This has now become a necessity because we have come to realise that we can neither get by with the segmented theories of the social sciences nor with those theoretical constructs which are entirely based on the social and historical experiences of a few industrialised Western societies. The more we realise that other societies have come through different kinds of development experiences, the more we feel intellectually obliged to come up with a commensurate cognitive effort so as to make them a part of an inclusive development theory construction. Towards such a goal our effort has to be exploratory and incremental.

There is much to learn by way of the experiences of the non-Western societies, and when the theoretical significance of such experiences is grasped fully, we shall have much to undo and redo in the corpus of our theoretical knowledge which is supposed to be about development. The challenge of knowing more about other societies, which we have ignored so far, is a basic challenge which has questioned the adequacy of our sensitivity and intellectual symbols to grasp and explain it. Once we have understood the challenge we should be able to come up with tentative, piecemeal, and incremental theoretical constructs about development, and then, at a later stage, engage in an inclusive cognitive effort to embrace *all* forms of development experience in reformulated theoretical constructs which can appropriately justify their claims to universal validity. Students of development process and development theory have, therefore, their work cut out for them.

I am grateful to Harvard University for renewing my status as a Visiting Scholar during the academic year of 1987–8 when I was struggling with the final draft of this manuscript. I owe a debt of gratitude to the Director and Fellows of the Center For International Affairs at Harvard for allowing me to become a part of their scholarly community. I am also grateful to the Social Sciences and Humanities Research Council of Canada for supporting my longitudinal field research for a number of years which helped me to understand the complexity of the development process first hand and then make it a part of my theoretical critiques and observations.

The librarians and staff of the universities of Harvard, Oxford, and Simon Fraser deserve my special thanks. Thanks are due to Anita Mahoney who helped me with the word processing of the manuscript. As in my other works, Geeta, my wife, who assisted me in editorial work, applied the strictest standard for clarity of expression but I could not always attain it. For the various shortcomings which still remain in this work, I alone am responsible.

A.H. Somjee
West Vancouver, 1990

1 Segmented Theories of Development

Different branches of human knowledge and, in particular, of the social sciences, have approached the study of the phenomena of development differently. In so doing they have also compartmentalised the various aspects of the development process so as to suit the peculiar demands of their own areas of specialisation. Such a compartmentalisation, and its resultant mutual isolation, were later on reinforced by specifically designed theories and intellectual approaches within each specialisation.

While from time to time, the specialists within each of the development compartments expressed their dissatisfaction with the arbitrariness of the intellectual boundaries drawn, they were, nevertheless, powerless against the drift of the discipline-oriented approaches to development studies. Some of them even felt that such compartmentalised approaches had become irreversible. Such a feeling often discouraged them from even trying to get out of the flow of the mainstream of intellectual activity in their respective disciplines and approaches to development studies.

Over the years, terms such as 'interdisciplinary approach' have lost their intellectual respectability and scholars have been advised not to stray away from the 'scientific' and 'rigorous' approaches developed by their own area of specialisation. Only stalwarts like Karl Marx, Max Weber, Fernand Braudel, Gunnar Myrdal, Bert Hoselitz, Albert Hirschman, Barrington Moore Jr and so on, have been connived at, and even condoned, for their excursions and trespasses into other areas. The rest are kept in line by means of an implied threat of the intellectual wilderness to which they could be consigned if they failed to apply disciplinary approaches and specialisation, and toe the established line.

In this chapter, we shall examine the approaches and standards laid down by the development purists and periodically, but ineffectively, challenged by the development interrelationists and integrationists. Implied in the position of the latter two is the contention that development phenomena, as a special field or fields, are the product of a number of interrelated factors and forces which

1

cannot always be sliced up to suit the specialist requirements of various disciplines and their specific theoretical approaches. It is argued that the continuing slicing up of the development process, beyond our initial analytical exercises, merely distorts our realistic understanding of its complexities and often undermines the very basis on which effective policies can be formulated.

The manner in which various disciplines have developed, and then been fortified by, their respective corpus of theoretical knowledge, allows us to zero in on common or related problems of development only as their specific branches view them. Under such constraints, development problems are not allowed to be viewed as problems belonging to phenomena of their own, but only as a part of the territory to which any specific discipline has extended. Consequently, in what we come to know about development, the disciplinary dimension, with all its limitations, is a major factor. Given such a development epistemology – the way we come to know about development – the disciplinary exclusivity becomes an important factor.

But more unhelpful than that, from the point of view of a broad approach to development studies, is the way in which theoretical knowledge in various branches of the social sciences has developed. Since such knowledge was developed in order that people might understand, and explain, the social and historical experiences of a few Western industrialised societies, and then extended, often without adequate refinement, to the attempted understanding of the non-Western societies, the very nature of such knowledge also becomes a factor in what we finally come to 'know' about developing societies.

In development studies we thus operate under two basic cognitive limitations: those which come from the segmented nature of the disciplines, imposing on us disciplinary perspectives; and the nature of theoretical knowledge which was developed in order to explain social and historical experiences of societies of a very different kind.

The theoretical knowledge about society, in particular, has not always been free from the accretions of time and place within which it was developed. Only a part of our knowledge about society can be abstracted from all its existential contexts and thus can be made free from its temporal and spatial accretions.

As a rule, the social sciences respond to any new area in which they take interest, as their 'new field', and depending upon the extent of interest in it among the scholarly community, the 'new field' may then become a disciplinary sub-field. Excursions into sub-fields, initially, almost always take place with the help of the existing theoretical resources of the discipline, resulting in an annexation of the new territory into the existing one.

That is what has happened to development studies. Portions of what may be regarded as the territory of development studies were incorporated into different disciplines so as to be intellectually pursued like any other parts of those disciplines.

Only in a handful of cases have scholars realised and, above all, given expression to the view that what has been sliced off, as a new territory to be added to the existing discipline, often leaves out a lot which cannot be brought within the conventional boundaries of various disciplines, and that serious intellectual problems present themselves, later on, in the piecing together of what was artificially cut asunder in the first place.

Simply put, the problem of the relationship between economic growth, as studied by economists, political development, as studied by political scientists, and social change, as studied by sociologists and anthropologists, becomes a nightmarish problem because of an initial, and artificial, slicing off, and then, subsequently, piecing together of various bits of the development process. And then comes an equally intractable problem of determining what is still unclaimed, and the residual portion of the territory of development studies.

Various branches of the social sciences, while examining specific aspects of the development process, also show, in different degrees, resistance to extending their cognitive effort to the understanding of closely related forces and elements which, traditionally speaking, do not fall within their own field of specialisation. Such a resistance to an extended effort is also in evidence even when it is clear that the very chopped-up nature of their disciplines – chopping up of all things a phenomenon like the development process – is arbitrary, and, in some eyes, epistemologically untenable.

What is thus injected into development studies is a concern for disciplinary jurisdiction, and fiefdom, rather than the perpetual sharpening of one's intellectual thrust. The fact that development phenomena are full of processes with their own antecedents, continuities, imbalances, consequences and so on, not all of which fall strictly within the discretely demarcated jurisdictions of disciplines, worries only a few practitioners of those disciplines.

The purity of the disciplinary approach, while examining various aspects of development, as stated earlier, is manifested in different

degrees by different branches of the social sciences. The greatest
degree of resistance to what is going on outside the traditional
confines of the disciplines is shown by economics, then to a lesser
degree by political science, and still less by sociology, and, perhaps,
the least by anthropology. Consequently the social sciences, have
been able to pay attention to the related aspects of development
phenomena in different degrees. But that is where their relative
advantage ends, so far as development studies are concerned. After
that they too couch their findings strictly within the theoretical
confines of their own disciplines. And unless and until development
studies themselves come into their own, with their own distinct
theoretical efforts, and cease to be adjuncts of various other
disciplines, the present situation is likely to continue.

Moreover, there is, so far, a limited intellectual exploration into
either the wider notion of development – including the field of
human social and political capacity, along with economic growth and
social equality – or into the treating of development as a broader,
and inclusive phenomenon, to balance out the earlier chopped up
approach. Since the emerging countries, for historical and social
reasons, have gone through prolonged periods of arbitrary and
discriminatory rule, which have stunted their all-round development,
we have also to think in terms of something as basic as human
development. For this we neither have enough sensitivity nor adequate intellectual tools.

Those and other issues will be discussed in this chapter. The
chapter is divided into the following parts: (I) the development
purists, (II) the development interrelationists, (III) the development
integrationists, (IV) the development expatriates, and (V) some
general observations. We shall now examine each of these in some
detail.

I THE DEVELOPMENT PURISTS

The unwillingness of the economists to go beyond the narrow
confines of their own discipline, even when they are dealing
with the development process, with all its mind-boggling multi-
dimensionality, partly rests on their anxiety of losing the 'rigorous'
and 'scientific' character of their own discipline. In the eighteenth and
nineteenth century, under the inspiration of the English Utilitarians
and classical economists, economics became a 'science', relegating

moral issues to philosophers, or whoever had the taste for them. Since then even as advisers to national and international organisations on policy matters, where moral choices are involved, the economists have continued to believe in the single dimensionality of their own discipline. Of all the social scientists, they are the least troubled by their own limitations even when they are engaged in different aspects of development studies.

Since the end of the Second World War, a large number of top-flight economists have been involved in generating perspectives and policies for helping out the developing countries. One of the earliest attempts in that connection was made by Paul Samuelson, who maintained that solutions to helping the developing countries out of their backwardness, could be found in free trade. He argued that through free trade, the developing countries would be able to market their commodities and manufactured goods in the developed countries, and that within a foreseeable future, the expanded export capability of the former would lead to a gradual increase in their wages and in their standard of living in general.

Samuelson was roundly criticised both by Raul Prebisch and Gunnar Myrdal for oversimplifying the complex problem of economic backwardness in developing countries and suggesting a solution which was entirely based on the experiences of a handful of industrially developed economies. For those two critics, the empirical evidence relating to Samuelson's prescription was the other way round. Such evidence suggested that the real benefit of free trade did not reach the poor wage earners in developing countries, but the middlemen in exporting as well as importing countries.

Then there were the Harrod-Domar model, Rosenstein-Rodan model, and the writings of Ragnar Nurske which tried to construct development policies, based on the experiences of industrially developed countries, applicable to the area of saving and capital accumulation. Once again, the historical and social contexts of the development of industrially advanced societies were ignored, and the prescriptions abstracted from their economic growth were presumed to have a universal applicability.

Apart from their insensitivity to cultural and social contexts within which some societies registered economic growth and others did not, these well-meaning scholars also overlooked the fact that their own theorisation of the experiences of the developed societies was what Lord Robbins called 'historico-relative'.[1] But such a warning fell on deaf ears. To most economists, economic growth was neither culture-specific nor a product of certain historical conditions and opportunities. For them it was subject to its own laws irrespective of the human, social, cultural or historical contexts within which economic growth, or the absence of it, occurred.

For such economists the problem was simply one of identifying the laws of the internal dynamics of economic growth, cracking their code, and using such knowledge to bring about economic growth elsewhere. Their effort was, therefore, not directed to a broader understanding of society, culture, human activity, political institutions, individual and group choices, all of which exert varying degrees of influence on economic growth itself, but was concerned merely with the laws to which economic growth was subject. To that extent economic activity had to be studied as a pure activity, unsullied by cultural, political, or moral considerations. Conversely, even in an apparent social mix, where different factors could be presumed to be present, it was always possible to identify, and abstract, that which was purely economic, and then discover what kind of laws it was subject to. Like pure economic growth, the laws which governed it had also to be stated in an equal degree of economic purity.

With such an intellectual ambition, what came handy to the economists studying growth was the abstract intellectual machinery of model-building, on the one hand, and mathematics, on the other. You could now use them to probe 'deeper', and sideways, into the complexity of pure economic growth. You could now also relate economic growth to similarly approached international dimensions of economic growth, trade, aid, and investment.[2]

A number of questions, however, continued to plague the development economists who took the purity route. Among others, the questions concerning what constitutes development itself often led to answers which abruptly stopped at economic indices. Even answers relating to equity in growth were couched, often hesitatingly, in pure economic terms. The only time when some development economists ventured to go out of their conventional definition of development, was when they viewed economic growth as primarily that which would serve 'the basic needs', as formulated by Streeten and Burki.[3]

Among the development economists, however, the testament of 'the basic needs' failed to arouse enough enthusiasm. For one thing these two development economists were asking a generation of economists, brought up on the purity of the discipline and a scientific infrastructure which had made economic science seem as 'scientific' as the natural sciences, to go to related areas of economic growth which would not only undermine the status of their scientific discipline but drop them in a sea of development complexity.

Moreover, the assumption behind 'the basic needs' was that once you made them a part of your development policy, and also provided the necessary funds for such a policy, the rest would take care of itself. What such an assumption overlooked was the fact that even if you did all that, you could not be sure either of the policy's implementation or of the benefit's reaching precisely all those who were targeted for it. The confidence of the economists either in the government machinery or in the bureaucracy of developing countries, of which they themselves periodically become a part, was clearly misplaced. In all emerging countries, there is a phenomenal growth of what may be regarded as development bureaucracy, and it often becomes a part of the problem rather than of its solution. Somewhere along the line not enough attention was paid to what in fact happens to all those good intentions in developing countries.

The fact of the matter is that most of those societies where basic needs are sought to be provided, also have deeply entrenched social inequality. And with that also goes the unequal political capacity to get equal benefits from the provisions of policy. There are specific social and historical reasons for it in every society, and we shall go into details of the differentiated political capacity in developing societies in subsequent chapters. Such a difference in political capacity ensures unequal gains even from those development policies which target only the disadvantaged sections of society.

Under those circumstances, officially and in terms of formal budgetary provisions and spending, so far as the books are concerned, the poor have been 'helped' several times over. And still the disadvantaged sections of those societies further deteriorate in their condition or remain where they were. The crucial question to ask, then, is how to implement a well-intentioned development policy so that its provisions reach precisely those segments of society which are targeted for them. And it is here that we come across wider issues which development economists hesitate to go into.

The idea is to identify not merely what needs to be done, but also how to go about doing it. As stated earlier, not all segments of developing societies are capable of uniform response to development stimuli. That means that before you embark on the implementation of a development policy you need to have a clear picture of the various unequal segments and factors which have inhibited responses to development stimuli in the past. Not all such inhibiting factors are economic in nature, nor can they be fixed only by means of an economic solution. Consequently, development strategies by their very nature have to be multi-dimensional and co-ordinated.

Such an approach would then necessarily take you to various development co-ordinates which are not confined to any single branch of the social sciences or human knowledge as such. With development goals formulated by the basic-needs economists, you need to understand the nature of social organisation, and the way in which it reinforces economic disparity, economic and cultural factors which give rise to different political capacities and attitudes to authority, especially on the part of the disadvantaged, which prevent them from becoming the demanders and takers of what has been earmarked for them in development policy.

Then there is the problem of the mobilisation of the disadvantaged in which social workers, political workers or non-government agencies are invariably involved. Thus, before you provide for the basic needs of everyone, and particularly of those who need them the most, there are a number of related problems to be looked into. But such related problems, alas, do not fit into the kind of intellectual framework which the conventional development economists have built for themselves.

The various co-ordinates of the development process are so deeply enmeshed in one another that the demands of specialised disciplines, in particular of development economics, to be able to continue their pure and 'scientific' character, begin to sound arbitrary and even simplistic. This is because we often slice, cut and chop development problems so as to suit the demands of our specialised disciplines, and our 'solutions', at the other end, are as fragmentally formulated, and distorted, as our understanding of those problems.

One of the basic problems that we face in our observation, analysis and strategy in development studies is the want of effort on our part at overcoming the limitations of our intellectual disciplines. While our social science disciplines, and their theoretical components, make special kinds of demands on us, in order to qualify as 'sciences' – strictly dealing with only those aspects which can be reduced to discrete variables and abstractions, and then become amenable to identification, measurement, and generalisation, all the imperatives of the natural sciences – the actuality of experiences in the field of development studies, after decades of what Paul Streeten called 'errors, false starts, and dead ends', point in the diametrically opposite direction. The latter inevitably brings in broader social, human, and moral issues which cannot be sliced and chopped so easily to suit the analytical and measuring imperatives of the disciplines which want to be 'scientific' in the same sense as the natural sciences are.

What we thus have by way of development studies is often a heap of unrelated and sliced-up disciplinary understandings and fragments, none of which by itself has significantly added to our overall understanding of the problem of development. Later on we shall examine the views of scholars who have sought to overcome the limitations imposed by various social science disciplines in development studies.

Political science too, like economics, has produced its own purists to look at the phenomena of political development. It is the oldest of the disciplines among the social sciences, with the most respectable intellectual pedigree (stretching back to Aristotle), and so political scientists have approached the study of the phenomena of political development in emerging societies with great intellectual self-confidence. For a long time they viewed the political process in developing countries as they were used to viewing it in developed countries, that is, as a separate phenomenon produced by political forces and their own internal dynamics. The independence, purity, and even primacy of politics, which are often taken for granted in the study of politics in Western countries, were now extended to the study of political development in emerging societies. Few works in the early phase acknowledged the fact that societal factors, including the economic, play a far greater role in political development process of those societies than was previously realised.

The 1960s and 1970s saw an explosion of books on political development. The bulk of those books assumed that the political development of developing societies could be studied with the help of theories, concepts and approaches developed by political science, and other related disciplines, for studying the industrialised societies of the West.

At a more personal level, the political scientists had watched, with great excitement, the rapidly changing political situation of the post Second World War period. They were deeply sympathetic to various national movements which had focussed on political independence from colonial rule. And some of those political scientists were also in close touch with the leaders of such movements. These included distinguished political scientists such as Harold Laski at the London School of Economics, Rupert Emerson at Harvard, and René Dumont at the Sorbonne. Those scholars had very much hoped that with the withdrawal of colonial rule, and with the establishment of liberal political institutions thereafter, the bulk of the problems of the ex-colonies would be taken care of. This was also the belief of their students, who led the various national movements: that with the help of such institutions they would be able to reconstruct their societies and economies in the shortest possible time. Some of them also believed that given the prior experiences of the industrially advanced countries – in the process of modernisation, industrialisation and development in general – they, the developing countries, would be able to avoid a blind trial-and-error process, and might even succeed in skipping the centuries in order to catch up with the West.

In their post-independence period, the leaders of the newly independent countries made a sincere attempt to emulate the various Western legal and political institutions, practices and ideals. But they soon realised that such borrowed institutions and practices also had to operate in environments that were culturally and socially very different.

The imported institutions, and their underlying normative structures, began interacting with the indigenous institutions and their normative structures, and thereby created an interactive complexity for which neither the discipline of political science, nor its practitioners, nor indeed the corpus of its theoretical knowledge, was prepared. The practitioners of the discipline, therefore, found the easiest way out (no matter how very inadequate), and that was to ignore whatever did not fit into their own preconceived theoretical frameworks. Very few took up the challenge of either getting down to refining that knowledge or of expressing its inadequacy so that at a future date such a task could be undertaken. The bulk of them viewed the complexity of political development in developing countries as similar to that which the Western countries had known and experienced in the early days of their parallel development.

Apart from the inadequacy of the existing theoretical knowledge, especially in the field of political development, what was also ignored was the fact that in developing countries the political development process could not be viewed in isolation from broad social and cultural contexts. Nor was there sufficient awareness of the fact that to try and understand such a process in pure political terms as we do in our efforts to understand the same in the developed countries, justifiably or otherwise, would not suffice. Some scholarly publications on political development paid lip service to social and cultural contexts, and then went on to apply the reigning models and approaches in the discipline, thus ensuring the continuity of the purist approach.

Let us now take a few representative samples of such works. In his *The Stages of Political Development* (1965), A.F.K. Organski[4] formulated his theory identifying the 'stages' in Western political development and then extended it to other regions of the world. Like W.W. Rostow he believed that all societies would go through a more or less similar process of development and that their politics would be dominated, sequentially, by similar issues. Organski, therefore, came out with his own list of issues round which the politics of nations would revolve, namely unification, industrialisation, welfare and abundance.

Apart from the implied universality and the sequence of 'stages', the politics concerning those issues, across nations, for Organski had very little to do with the particular historical and cultural background of those countries. For him the issues which fuelled the politics of various stages were not only identical, but were also unmixed by other considerations, despite the fact that both in their sources and consequences they affected other areas.

The purity of political development approach came out much more strongly in the writings of Gabriel Almond and Lucian Pye. Almond began by formulating a theory which could help him identify 'political systems differing radically in scale, structure, and culture'.[5] Earlier he had come to the conclusion that the cultural dimension played an important part in the political process of developing societies. Consequently he had paid a lot of attention to the writings of sociologists and anthropologists. But the towering scholar who presided over the search for new sociological approaches in the 1950s was Talcott Parsons. Even Almond, in search of the social and cultural bases of politics, especially in developing areas, could not escape his influence. Instead of going into the cultural complexities of any particular society, Almond borrowed what was readily available and, in particular, Parsons's much talked-about (at that time) theory of 'pattern-variables'.

The Parsonian theory provided a classificatory tool for pigeon-holing societies, as 'modern' and 'traditional'. Parsons's theory could have been used as a speculative or analytical theory for an initial exploration awaiting further refinement by means of actual field research. A lot of internal differences within what he regarded as the 'modern' and the 'traditional' should have been grasped first, and then, without taking the pejorative position of viewing everything 'traditional' as backward, he could have persuaded a generation of scholars, waking up to the realities of the emerging world in the 1950s, to go into the *actual* complexities, rather than the presumed characteristics, of those emerging societies, and come up with a sensitive and nuanced social analysis. This was not done, however.

But apart from the distorting impact of the Parsonian 'pattern-variables', Almond began to view the political system as a kind of arena which was concerned, primarily, with the 'politics' of what was put into it and what came out of it. Under those circumstances the political system itself was going to be concerned with the management, not of social and economic forces, but only of political forces. Both inputs and outputs into the political system, from his point of view, were largely political. Such a notion of a political system, where politics are all about political factors, was highly inadequate as a tool of analysis. It was, in fact, anchored in an equally questionable premise that the politics of the Western societies are only about political matters and can therefore be examined by means of a purely political approach.

One of the much discussed works in political development is *The Civic Culture* (1963).[6] In that work the authors sought to develop a common framework for evaluating what they called in the subtitle 'political attitudes and democracy in five nations'. The countries compared were as diverse as Britain, the USA, Germany, Italy and Mexico. There again, the comparison remained purely at a political level. What had happened to Germany and Italy, before the Second World War, was, as matter of fact, deeply rooted in the social and economic conditions generated by the earlier period. Moreover, in the case of Germany in particular, her own economic history, ever since she had become a modern nation, was a powerful factor in influencing her social organisation as well as her politics. The same was true, to a large extent, of Italy. Mexico, on the other hand, required a far deeper understanding of her culture and society, together with her economic relationship with the United States.

Looking back one feels that the students of political development, schooled in the approaches of viewing politics as an unmixed phenomenon, had to go through a period of trial and error to realise, later on, that their neglect of the related areas – economic, social and cultural –

especially in a field such as the political development process, caused a distortion in their own approaches.

Another major work, cast in a similar intellectual tradition, was Lucian Pye's *Aspects of Political Development* (1966).[7] For Pye the crucial factor in the political development of a nation is how well it succeeds in generating political participation and equality, on the one hand, and institutional capability and political accommodation, for conceding major demands without disruption, towards a common political advancement, on the other.

From the point of view of the political development process, these are perhaps the most crucial goals. And Pye was fully justified in pointing out their central role in the political development process of any particular society. For his part, Pye derived his understanding of those goals from what the founding fathers of American political institutions had debated, agonised over, and finally enshrined in the constitution. Such an early, institutionalised provision for those goals deeply influenced the American political character and her political process in general.[8] Nevertheless, the very analysis and treatment of such highly influential goals were couched, alas, exclusively in pure political terms.

American politics then, as now, was deeply enmeshed in the economic and social forces of the colonial and post-colonial society, and one of the remarkable achievements of the leading public figures, of the first few decades of the post-independence period, was the successful steering of the political process towards the attainment, in actual operational terms, of those goals.

The purists in political development, as in economic growth, thus derived their understanding, and perspectives, on development from the historical experiences of a few Western societies. Not much was added to them even when understanding of the non-Western societies gradually increased, largely through the efforts of different disciplines. After an initial exploration, what stood in the way of further development in our cognitive effort was the controversial notion that since Western economic and political phenomena could be studied with the help of the exclusive approaches which the social sciences had developed, one could do the same so far as the corresponding development phenomena of the emerging societies were concerned. That indeed was an error. More about it later.

Of the various branches of the social sciences, anthropology is least inclined to view social change, or its equivalent of development, from a puristic point of view. In their attempt to understand social change, anthropologists routinely include a wide range of factors such as cultural, economic, political and historical, and often view it as a complex interaction of all these.

That however is not the case with anthropology's closely allied discipline, sociology. Sociology at different stages of its growth has often sought to look at the problem of social change from the perspective of the social system *per se*, often to the exclusion or diminution of other factors. That is particularly true of the purists within the discipline. In their way of thinking, changes first of all hit the functioning social systems and then are reflected in their sub-systems or related systems as a consequence. Under those circumstances, non-social forces, such as economic, political or educational, are viewed as sub-social forces first, and then credited with the ability to affect the wider system.

The very intellectual construction of social system, and the relegating of other systems to the level of sub-system or less, is often drawn from the identifiable amalgam of institutions and practices of a few industrialised Western societies, and then woven into neat systemic patterns. Such a systemic approach is then extended to the analysis of non-Western societies, where the tenuous linkages between various sub-systems of extended family, kinship, ethnicity, religion, economy, politics and so on, create, at best, a segmented social system, with a mind-boggling problem of identifying operational relationships between its segments. Only through a neat reductionist exercise can they be reduced to parts of a functioning whole. But then it becomes an intellectual exercise in gross oversimplification, often discouraging attempts to know more about the complexities and relationships among different segments.

Such a shortcoming, when viewed from the point of view of development studies – where you desperately look for effective social dimensions to supplement understanding of economic growth and political development – negates sociology's intellectual value. While you yearn to get a glimpse of the *actual* conditions which serve as a backdrop to your cognitive effort, what you actually get through such systemic approaches are neatly packaged abstract arguments claiming universal validity.

The sociologists were in such a great hurry to undertake 'the goal of scientific activity' (defined as one which consists of advancing 'variable propositions concerning the relations among variables'9) that either they did not pay much attention to the basic difference among societies, or they thought that mere theory construction rather than its instrumental value was their primary concern. The students of social change among them did not make much progress after the initial effort at theory construction by stalwarts such as Marx, Weber and Parsons. And the dissatisfied among them swung to the other extreme of descriptive empiricism, restricting the importance of their work to the themes and issues which they examined rather than also bringing to bear the significance of their work to theory refinement.

One of the greatest theorists to think through the continuum of society – economy – polity, was Karl Marx. Social classes for Marx were structured on their economic base, which in turn determined the nature of political relationship in society. While in Marx's writing the complex interplay of these remained unmistakable, he nevertheless expressed their interactions, by and large, in economic terms. Subsequently, Marx's *tour de force* at theory construction was reproduced by social change purists in their comprehensive systems very much in the tradition of grand theories.

For their construction of highly ambitious and comprehensive social systems the post-Weber sociologists went back to Marx. Marx's approach to the continuum of society – economy – polity was now expressed in the new form of 'social system'. And those who rejected the regenerative role which Marx had accorded to conflicts, substituted equilibrium as the goal of all systems. Thus in the place of Marx's predominantly economic system, what we came to have was an equally subsuming social system.

Unlike Marx, Max Weber wanted his readers to pay special attention to the differences among societies before embarking upon ambitious theory construction which embraced all of them. Through his writings on social history and social theory, both of which were cast within highly developed methodological frameworks, Weber tirelessly reminded scholars of the immense diversity and plurality of human cultural, economic, political and legal institutions. For him most societies were the products of their unique historical and social experiences, values, institutions and practices. He argued that to find *a common ground* among them – so that we may interject our methodological niche among them, and then go on to theory construction based on our own historical and empirical research and analysis – was replete with the danger of oversimplification, pseudo parallelisms, and assumed universalisms.

Weber was quick to realise the inability of his colleagues who came from history or economics or social theory to cope with the cognitive challenge thrown at them by the problem of *pluralism*. The philosophical writings of William James had sensitised scholars, especially of the post-First World War period, of the need to go beyond a conception of social reality which had been regarded as what he called 'the block universe'. This was then reinforced by the discovery and understanding of other cultures and their institutions by anthropologists, historians, linguists and philosophers. But while the uncomfortable philosophers, facing the challenge of pluralism, could reason their way back into monistic positions – by emphasising the need to have universal standards of judging the truth, and of determining it by commonly accepted canons of reasoning – social historians and theorists could not. The latter two were now left to their own intellectual resources, either to reason themselves out of such situations, or to build an awareness of social pluralism. They also had to provide a commensurate theoretical argument to make pluralism look intellectually respectable, and then await the moral and intellectual support of their fellow scholars. In respect of the latter position, of making scholars aware of the challenges of pluralism, and the cognitive and methodological obligations which such a position generated, the contribution of Max Weber was second to none.

But Max Weber was also aware of the fact that scholars often started off with a pluralistic ambition and then moved to a more manageable universalistic position, simply because there was not much in the corpus of theoretical knowledge to support such a position. For historical and social pluralism, much greater theoretical support was needed than what had hitherto been available. Conversely, inductive research incursions into those fields needed a bold theoretical feed-back and refinement. None of this was forthcoming. In terms of sheer intellectual hazards, monistic positions had the security not only of tradition but also of numbers, for few, if any, wanted to take the pluralist route right down the line.

Max Weber's final work, *General Economic History*, which was posthumously published, was devoted to such concerns.[10] Armed with his own phenomenal scholarship and research into various belief-systems, social organisations, economic and political institutions (a life-time pursuit in itself), and an incomparable capability to put all these in highly sophisticated and insightful theoretical arguments, Weber had built a case for historical and social pluralism and, to a lesser extent, for theories to interpret them. In fact it was his hope that as scholarship of the former grew, so would the theoretical knowledge needed to interpret it.

Unfortunately, at the hands of succeeding scholars in sociology, and in particular of Talcott Parsons, who himself had done so much to introduce Max Weber to the Anglo-Saxon world, the Weberian pluralistic emphasis did not receive adequate attention. Nor did it become an area of research priority with scholars whom Weber influenced. After Weber only the anthropologists, and some social theorists with a taste for epistemological questions arising out of increasing knowledge of different cultures, continued to take interest in social pluralism, both within and among societies.

For one thing, Talcott Parson's own theory of 'pattern variables', of dividing societies into pairs of opposites – such as traditional or modern, functionally diffused or specific, ascription or achievement oriented, and particularistic or universalistic – became a substitute for empirical research into the actual differences among societies. Before the very start of one's research, societies were so branded that all that one had to do by way of 'research' was to further rationalise such distinctions. Different societies had to be fitted into the predetermined categories, with little or no room for the grey area between them. And what was worse, instead of more knowledge about the complexity of social change in different societies, and the discovery of specific causal and other kinds of explanations for it, what often came out at the other end was a repeated 'confirmation' of a doubtful theory.

Thus the social-change theorists of purist persuasion provided less and less explanation of the phenomena of social change with reference to different societies, and provided more and more arguments deduced from extraneous models of the social system. And since there was little scope in such models to explain anything except with reference to an all-embracing social system, other factors received minimal attention.

The development purists in three major branches of the social sciences thus looked at the phenomenon of the development process, and the complex range of issues involved in it, essentially from the perspectives of their own disciplines and through abstractions of specific themes and issues in which they had specialist interest. In a sense what they were doing was not development studies but incorporating chunks of them into their respective territories, and then examining them as parts of their own disciplines. What was, therefore, introduced into development studies was not only discipline-oriented segmentation but also its own irreconcilability with other similar segments. The purists in those branches would have little or nothing to do with corresponding efforts in cognate disciplines. With a few exceptions, they either ignored or derided the scholars across the disciplinary fence even when the latter, were dealing with closely related or similar issues. And those who dared defy such rigid boundaries risked intellectual isolation. Only the few with high intellectual stature were forgiven for wanting to cross the disciplinary fence. To them and their efforts we now turn.

II THE DEVELOPMENT INTERRELATIONISTS

Let us now briefly examine the efforts of some of those scholars who, in all the sub-fields of development – economic growth, political development and social change – tried to transcend the segmentary divisions imposed on them by their respective disciplines. This they did by going in search of interrelations between those segments. Among scholars engaged in relating the phenomenon of economic growth to political development and social change, there were some who wanted to come up with a fresh perspective on their interrelationships, and others who merely wanted to amalgamate the existing segmentary theoretical approaches. In this section we shall examine both groups.

Karl Marx, as we noted in the earlier section, looked at economic development from a broad social and historical perspective. For him the economic organisation of society was a part of its wider social and historical continuum. The economic structure of society, as implicit in its productive relationships, exercised a deterministic influence on its political relationships, the nature of laws, and cultural values in general.

Such a perception of their interrelations was then worked out by Marx round his specific concern, namely social inequality. For him the social inequality which is implicit in different forms of productive relationships at different stages in social and economic history also manifests itself in the structure of laws, nature of social institutions, and preferences in value systems.

In such a situation of interrelatedness, the importance of the economic relationship was paramount to Marx, and the rest of the fields either reflected or reinforced such a social reality. Since the economic relationship was the primary reason for social inequality, its solution for Marx was also in that field. Once that was attended to, the rest would fall into in place.

The interrelationist theory of Marx, implicit in his views on social inequality, where different forces reflected or reinforced the reality of economic relationship, has received much less attention at the hands of scholars than other themes and issues which he addressed. In reaching such a conclusion, Marx attributed the power of fundamental change to economic forces and relations, thereby making other forces either reflect such a reality or reinforce it. There was thus no discord among them. The reflective or the subordinate character of other forces to the economic also took away the need to build, so far as Marx was concerned, a new theory of interrelations and sequences. For him such interrelations, and their social and political consequences, inevitably followed the economic.[11]

Max Weber, in a sense, continued and extended the approach of Marx, of building general arguments and theories which explained the interconnectedness of various social processes giving rise to specific types of economic growth, political system, and social organisation. But Weber was also keen on going deeper than Marx in identifying the interrelationships between different social processes which cut across the rigid boundaries of economic structure, political system and social organisation. Unlike Marx, who had put economic and non-economic forces in a rigid determining-determined framework, Weber assiduously tried to point out, with the help of his enormous scholarship and grasp of social history, how no single set of forces enjoyed predominance at all times. He believed that we need to cultivate much greater sensitivity to the shifting scene of influences in social history, and bring to bear the significance of such an understanding to our exercises in theory construction.

Since in Weber's time, and before him, in Marx's, the development process was sought to be explained through the idiom of the growth of capitalism, the former painstakingly related the influence of the variety of social and historical forces which shaped different kinds of capitalism in history. By so doing, Weber introduced yet another dimension to his approach to the study of the development process, that is, the interconnectedness of social forces.

Added to his emphasis on historical and empirical pluralism, which we discussed earlier, the interconnectedness of social forces made on him a near-impossible demand in theory construction which could attend to both those concerns. In effect he had deprived himself of the convenient tool of reductionism which made such an intellectual exercise simpler and more manageable. While he did not succeed fully in responding to the challenge of building a common theoretical framework within which the above-mentioned concerns could be addressed, he nevertheless left behind a legacy of intellectual explorations which are as educative in what they did not achieve as in what they did.

Weber believed that various religions, during certain historical periods, in a unique fashion shaped the attitude to life, economic activities and their goals, in different societies.[12] In the course of time economic forces began to exercise an equally determining influence, along with religion in certain societies. Together, they helped to crystallise the ethical system, implicit in religions, so that it in turn influenced the emerging legal and political institutions.

In order to illustrate this point, Weber made a bold attempt at identifying 'the economic ethic' of the major religions such as Confucianism, Hinduism, Buddhism, Judaism, Christianity and Islam. Their economic ethic, according to him, seems to have shaped the orientation to economic action of their followers. Weber, however, was careful enough not to claim a causal relationship between the two, but such an ethic, nevertheless, was of paramount importance to him among the forces competing for influence.

In his seminal work, *The Protestant Ethic and the Spirit of Capitalism*, Weber underlined the effect of various Puritan denominations, in particular Calvinism, which turned the pursuit of wealth, for their followers, from a mere 'advantage' to a 'duty'. Weber thus 'canonised', as R.H. Tawney put it, the 'economic virtue', making 'capitalism . . . the social counterpart of Calvinist theology'.[13]

In his final work, *General Economic History*, Weber examined the nature of various social, economic, and political institutions in Western Europe which had facilitated the growth of capitalism in various societies. Furthermore, he had earlier pointed out how the social background of capitalism in different societies had influenced the operation of its various institutions. Weber had later on broadened the 'background' argument to include land tenure systems, guilds and commerce, together with the peculiarities of administrative structure, urban civilisation, system of laws, and so on. He then had underscored the need to undertake a nuanced historical and social analysis of the relationship between such background forces and the kind of social organisation that they gave rise to.[14]

Finally, Weber's theory of institutions put a great emphasis on the contextual factors which gave rise to those institutions and influenced the manner in which they operated. For him, the social and historical contexts also gave those institutions a definite direction and helped crystallise their equally specific functions.[15]

For Weber, as Parsons put it, what needs to be grasped, to begin with, is 'the fundamental variability of social institutions'. Furthermore, 'the institutional system of the modern Western world is not a 'natural order' which has come about by the mere process of removal of obstacles' but represents 'one of several possible lines of social development'. And by the same token 'radically different structures, such as those found in the great oriental civilizations are not 'arrested stages' in a development leading in the same direction, but are simply different'.[16]

Let us now examine some of the efforts made by the economists who tried to go beyond the narrow confines of their disciplines while grappling with the phenomenon of development. In their *Society, Politics and Economic Development* (1967), Erma Edelman and Cynthia Morris felt that one of the ways to transcend the limitations of their own discipline in development studies was to make 'an attempt to bridge the gap between theory and practice of economic development by means of a systematic statistical analysis of social, political, and economic characteristics of nations' at different stages of their development.[17] The authors also believed that economic growth may or may not always go with a corresponding socio-political development. We therefore need to understand not only the relationship between different phenomena in the process of development, but also how different combinations of variables give a clue to their relationships within such a process.

Then there was the problem of the way in which various disciplines collected their material on developing countries. As opposed to economics, with its masses of quantified data, those collected by political science and sociology/anthropology were either purely descriptive or descriptive with different degrees of analysis. How do we then relate one to the other?

Such a problem, as we saw earlier, did not arise in the case of Max Weber in his effort to relate the rise of capitalism to the socio-religious conditions of different denominations of Protestantism. This was largely due to the fact that his economic data itself was cast in the format of qualitatively analysed historical material. Such an approach even facilitated Weber's excursions into similar relationships between different belief systems and the economic organisations which they influenced and shaped in different societies.

Edelman and Morris, however, wanted the same kind of statistical 'precision' in disciplines to be used in development studies, as exists in economics. Such a precision, they believed, ought not to be sacrificed even when one was relating certain aspects of development phenomena studied differently by different disciplines.[18]

The cost of such a demand for exact knowledge, enabling interrelationships to be located statistically between various aspects of the development process, was very high indeed. At the very start you had to ignore all those complexities within the development process which did not lend themselves to a simple statistical treatment, and also ignore all those interrelationships themselves which posed a similar problem for statistical analysis. But even if you did reduce such complexities to suit the limitation of your statistical method, much of what you had set out to understand in terms of interrelationships would have been lost.

At the root of the problem, there was the inability of the authors to come to grips with the two kinds of empirical tools with which social scientists deal – descriptive and statistical – and their respective advantages and limitations. Descriptive empiricism may reveal many of the complexities of actual situations but it can also, simultaneously, defy any attempt at numerical interrelations between aspects of the development process. At the other extreme, statistical empiricism can help you to be more 'exact', at least in a postulational sense, but the resulting material may only be a series of deductions from values that you attributed to the complex phenomena in the first place. In the empiricism of the latter variety you have the assurance of deductive reasoning, but this depends on a series of assumptions that were made at the start of your chain of reasoning. And as the deductive reasoning progresses, with its impressive statistical tables, it is tempting not to go back to those initial assumptions.

One of the basic problems which confronts interrelationists is the fact that the most worthwhile, and dependable, material about the society and politics of developing countries is in the form of social and cultural anthropology material, on the one hand, and of the history of institutions, together with description and analysis of political process, on the other. Such a material remains in the form of descriptive material and in recent years, many institutions devoted to development studies have also begun to recognise their value. Not all aspects of such material are amenable to a statistical resolution.

The problem of development interrelationships thus inevitably takes us to the fundamental problems of not only the segmentation of portions of development studies by various disciplines, but also the variety of intellectual tools developed by them to collect their data, which they present in an almost unrelatable condition.

Another major attempt in economics, at identifying development interrelations, is Everett Hagen's *On the Theory of Social Change: How Economic Growth Begins* (1962). It is the product of an attempt by an individual scholar to combine the insights, perspectives, and theoretical formulations dealing with development studies within different branches of the social sciences, to overcome the problems of an interdisciplinary approach. For such a purpose, he wrote, he had to 'master the literature on psychology, anthropology, and sociology'.[19]

In the early 1960s there was the hope that the several pieces of disciplinary research would move closer to one another, especially where common themes and issues concerning development were involved. It was hoped that from such a proximation would result a common framework for 'empirical investigation', and 'concept formation' to guide it. Such an intellectual evolution in development studies, however, did not materialise. The unintegrated perspectives, approaches, theoretical formulations, and so on, convinced the author of the truth of that much quoted statement by Hans Sachs, that 'the best interdisciplinary work is that which goes on within one skull.'[20]

In his own search for an interdisciplinary answer to the question of what prevents economic growth, Hagen came to the conclusion that 'economic obstacles' often constituted one of the minor problems and that the major problems came from personality formation and social conditions affecting economic growth. He therefore wanted to bring into his consideration of economic growth the part played by social – psychological factors.

To Hagen, a part of the problem was in the fact that social scientists, in particular in economics, keep looking at the natural sciences as the model of advancement of knowledge. But the natural sciences as compared to the social sciences are 'absurdly simple'. Moreover, the social sciences as compared to the natural sciences are still in their infancy.[21]

For Hagen, the developments in sociology of the 1950s and the 1960s were of special significance to development studies. Sociology during those decades was engaged in developing 'analytical models' which were able to take the discipline from classification to its next logical step, namely the identification of 'the functioning interactive elements'. Such a step would then help the discipline, and also development studies in general, to engage in 'generalization about functioning itself'.[22]

Hagen's faith in 'analytical models' built by sociologists was misplaced. Many such models were either lost in highly wordy and jargonised presentations or were too ethnocentric in their bias to become a means of understanding the complexities of non-Western societies. Others, being simply classificatory, were therefore of limited value. Moreover, whatever is analytically formulated, much in advance of the basic understanding of other societies, loses its intellectual credibility from the very start.

Furthermore, Hagen's fascination for a systemic approach, as adopted by economists and psychologists, did not bear the intended results in development studies. In the latter the nagging question was how much did the systemic approach, as a tool of analysis, help to identify the actual complexity of the development process? The answer was, not very much, unless background knowledge of the forces which affected the development process was available. Hagen was also overly optimistic when he maintained that systemic analysis could help in the formulation of causal explanations. In his words, 'I suggest that the understanding of causal relationships among the phenomena in the social sciences has reached a point at which there is no excuse for not employing the power of system analysis.'[23]

Over quarter of a century after the publication of Hagen's highly optimistic book on development interrelations, scholars would settle even for correlationships between descriptive and statistical or analytical materials, if only they could find them in development studies, let alone causal relationships between them. Even the very respectability of interdisciplinary approaches in development studies, as Michael Lipton points out, is far from established.[24] And so far as causal relationships in development studies are concerned, scholars in the field, realising the need to know much more about the complex terrain of the development process, and also the need to develop adequate conceptual tools to study it, have learned to regard them as a distant, very distant, goal.

Let us now briefly examine the corresponding attempts at identifying interrelated structures in the growth of political institutions, as presented by economic and political historians and political sociologists. One of the seminal works in that category is *Social Origins of Dictatorship and Democracy* (1966), by Barrington Moore Jr.[25] Moore went into the economic history of industrialised and industrialising societies, so as to identify the emergence of economic and political institutions and the interrelations between them. In order to build his thesis, Moore zeroed in on those economic forces, from the seventeenth to the twentieth century, which contributed to what he called a thrust towards economic modernisation. In such a thrust the relationship between the 'two classes' (the landed class and peasantry, in varying form) produced different kinds of political institutions in different societies. Those classes, together or separately, in their thrust towards economic modernisation, produced a variety of liberal democracies, communisms, and fascisms.

For Moore, the legal and political institutions of different countries were influenced and shaped by the two classes to facilitate their own drive towards economic development. In Britain, the US and France, he argued, there was some measure of co-operation, albeit different in nature, between the two classes. It was this co-operation which was able to produce different kinds of liberal political institutions in those countries. In Russia and China, on the other hand, after a prolonged period of stagnation, the peasantry, imbued with the spirit of radical change, and in conjunction with workers and other smaller classes, produced their respective brands of economic modernisation under communism. Finally, the thrust towards economic development in Germany and Japan came from the top, from the Prussian Junkers and the Samurais respectively, and produced different varieties of fascism.

By means of his historical scholarship, Moore documented the part played by the two classes in economic development, the nature of their relationship, and the resultant legal and political institutions. To such a framework of development interrelationships, Moore admitted, India was an exception. India had been able to industrialise herself, and also establish her liberal political institutions, without significant assistance from those two classes.

Moore's historical model, with all its interrelationist arguments, was only helpful in explaining the economic and political development of the countries of the Western world and, to a limited extent, Japan. Such a model, when extended to one of the major developing societies, namely India, began to appear inadequate. Moore's interrelationist model thus needed more than he could provide, and remained limited in value so far as the developing countries were concerned.

S.M. Lipset in his *The Political Man* (1963),[26] claimed that there was a positive relationship between the sustaining of liberal democratic institutions in various parts of the world and their social and economic bases. He argued that democratic institutions often go with a higher standard of living, education, urbanisation, and social organisations with particular kinds of characteristics.

Lipset's work led to a spate of research, trying to establish empirically such a relationship. The most interesting was Phillips Cutright's attempt at developing an index which could empirically establish the interdependence of political development, economic growth, educational attainments, urban development and communication facilities.[27]

Lipset's as well as Cutright's work ran into difficulty. Critics raised the question whether the 'correlates' and 'congruences' also meant 'causal' relationships between social bases and political development.[28] Moreover, enough evidence could be provided to support the contrary argument. Poor countries like India and Sri Lanka had democracy whereas wealthy countries like Kuwait and South Korea did not.

Such a controversy did not discourage Lipset. Instead of making his interrelations thesis more sophisticated, he, along with Smelser, went on to add a few more indices of development. In *Social Structure and Mobility in Economic Development* (1966), they argued that a simultaneous increase in many indices such as 'output per capita, political participation, literacy', is indicative of 'development' that has taken place. Such indices are accompanied by changes in social structure, education, urbanisation and so on.[29]

This work in interrelationships was cast in the earlier tradition of correlates and congruences. What was missing in it, nevertheless, was an intensive analysis of any specific area, indicating how in fact, in the process of development, the various indices which they had identified had actually correlated in a specific fashion, and not merely appeared in statistical correlation boxes.

III   THE DEVELOPMENT INTEGRATIONISTS

This brings us to yet another group of scholars: those who believe that by way of our meaningful perspectives on development, we need to go beyond not only the segmented approaches of development scholars but also those who have attempted historical and statistical correlations between development and various indices. Instead, they argue that through a process of integration of various aspects, we should be able to refer to certain *inclusive* dimensions of development which have been arbitrarily chopped up to suit the specialist requirements of certain social science disciplines. Such inclusive dimensions would no doubt differ from scholar to scholar; nevertheless, they would shift the discussion to what constitutes development itself from what the discipline-embedded approaches have to say about it in a fragmented fashion. Instead of viewing development as economic growth, political development, or social change, as we are used to doing, and then worrying about interrelations among them, why not view development as something that falls within its own inclusive category? That will then compel us to think about development across the disciplinary fences, perspectives, and theoretical divisions.

In this section we shall examine the views of scholars with such a broad approach to development studies. In that connection we shall refer to the ideas of Schumpeter, Myrdal, Hirschman, Hoselitz, Huntington and Nelson, Sen and Streeten. We will also consider the roles of anthropology, sociology and political science.

Joseph Schumpeter repeatedly warned his students of economics not to think of development as a segmented process but one which is essentially a part of the larger social process and needs to be considered as such. In his words: 'the social process is really one indivisible whole. Out of its great stream the classifying hand of the investigator artificially extracts economic facts.'[30]

Schumpeter, therefore, wanted his students to go back, as it were, to the social contexts of the 'abstracted' facts, at some stage of their analysis. From his point of view such a going back was of crucial importance before the students reached the ultimate goal of their intellectual endeavour, namely the building of 'causal' explanations and relationships. Such causal explanations must refer to the non-economic factors or else they would fall short of realistic social contexts. In his words:

> When we succeed in finding a definite causal relation between two phenomena, our problem is solved if the one which plays the 'causal' role is non-economic. We have then accomplished what we, as economists, are capable of in the case in question, and we must give place to the other disciplines. If, on the other hand, the causal factor itself is economic in nature, we must continue our explanatory effort until we ground upon a non-economic bottom. This is true for general theory as well as for concrete causes.[31]

For Schumpeter, then, one of the causal factors in economic analysis has to be non-economic. He took such a position to put across the view that economic activity has non-economic antecedents or consequences or both, and that one cannot be 'scientific' by abstractly attributing a causal position to economic factors when in actual fact such a position does not exist. He argued that one should be able to do one's economic analysis in conjunction with other factors, reflecting the true relative importance of both in the actual situation, or else one would not have undertaken a truly scientific analysis.

Schumpeter even took a definitive non-economic position to explain economic phenomena, which was close to Max Weber's general argument on economic change. In Schumpeter's words: '. . . it is not possible to explain *economic* change by previous economic conditions alone. For the economic state of a people does not emerge simply from the preceding economic conditions, but only from the preceding total situation.'[32]

Schumpeter's words fell on deaf ears. In the 1930s, and in the aftermath of the Second World War, there was a further segmentation between the social science disciplines, and in development studies in general. Nevertheless, Schumpeter's emphasis on the social whole, as constituting the background of conceptual analysis and theoretical arguments, was important. For it then became a focal point for subsequent development scholars to go back to.

Gunnar Myrdal was one of the few economists to raise the question of non-economic factors directly impinging upon the development process of emerging societies more than they do in industrially developed countries. Along with that he also raised the question of the inadequacy of the body of theoretical knowledge, even for the study of the economics and politics of industrially developed societies, let alone those of emerging countries.

Myrdal expressed those views quite persuasively and in detail, in his volume *An Approach to Asian Drama* (1970). In it he argued that unlike the process of economic growth in industrially developed societies – where social and cultural forces have become 'permissive' of economic growth, or at any rate the former adjust to the latter – the development process of emerging societies is deeply enmeshed in a variety of cultural and social forces. He called these latter forces 'institutional structure'. In his words:

> Conditions in the rich Western countries today are such that, broadly speaking, the social matrix is permissive of economic development or, when not, becomes readily readjusted so as not to place much in the way of obstacles in its path. This is why an analysis in 'economic' terms, abstracting from that social matrix, can produce valid and useful results. But that judgment cannot be accurately applied to South Asian conditions. Not only is the social and institutional structure different from the one that has evolved in Western countries, but, more important, the problem of development in South Asia is one calling for induced changes in that social and institutional structure, as it hinders economic development and as it does not change spontaneously, or, to any very large extent, in response to policies restricted to the 'economic' sphere.[33]

Myrdal thus viewed the development process as a part of the larger social process, requiring more inclusive development policies than the ones that were directed to what could be abstractedly called 'economic', at least in the context of developing countries. And he repeatedly urged scholars working on developing societies to go into the hitherto unexplored area of actual relationships between such forces in the process of development. He warmly welcomed the works of those scholars who tried to identify broader social and cultural forces operating behind economic and political institutions.[34]

Myrdal was also deeply concerned with the neglect of values and preferences in the 'science' of economics. For values and preferences orient and direct our economic activity. Myrdal maintained that in order to qualify as a 'science', economics had paid too heavy a price. In all his writings, therefore, he repeatedly criticised the positivistic and reductionist position of economics. Such a position, he said, comes up with distorted explanations when applied to the development process of emerging societies, where values, and even traditional values, play an inordinately important role.

Earlier, in his *Political Element in the Development of Economic Theory* (1930), Myrdal had criticised the drift of economics away from what he thought were the basic issues of policy, preference, and values. Those he maintained were implicit in most forms of economic activity. Subsequently, in his two seminal works, *American Dilemma* (1944) and *The Asian Drama* (1968), Myrdal tried to point out how much values and preferences were at the root of the economic and social policy needed to address the problems of those regions.[35]

After those two major bouts of empirical research, Myrdal's own position on development studies began to crystallise. He became increasingly critical of the total neglect of social and institutional (cultural) factors, which he believed to be crucial to the development process of emerging countries. What had made scholars insensitive to their presence, he argued, was the corpus of theoretical knowledge in the social sciences, in particular, in economics. For him its 'Euro-centricity' and suitability to advanced industrial societies, had made it quite 'inadequate to the reality' of underdeveloped societies.

Myrdal was highly suspicious of a number of concepts used in economic analysis, such as employment, unemployment, income, consumption, savings, investment, capital, output, capital/output ratio and so on. He felt that those concepts, on closer scrutiny, were still less helpful in examining the economic reality of developing societies.[36]

He often exhorted his readers to break out of the narrow disciplinary confines so as to be able to view problems of development from a more inclusive and realistic perspective. Since various branches of human knowledge had pursued the course of their specialist interests wherever their own search for truth and reliable knowledge took them, the students of development studies had an additional problem on their hands: that of bringing together various aspects of such knowledge 'in their mutual relationships' so as to be able to zero in, more effectively, on their own specific problems. For that purpose, Myrdal listed a number of disciplines and areas: 'history and politics, theories and ideologies, economic structure and levels, social stratification, agriculture, industry, population developments, health and education etc.'[37]

With Albert Hirschman came an unqualified expression of discontent with economic science and its approach to development studies. In the preface to his much discussed *Essay in Trespassing: Economics to Politics and Beyond* (1981), he quoted a line from the 1979 Report of the Russell Sage Foundation: '". . . the discipline [of economics] became professionally more narrow at precisely the moment when the problem [of development] demanded broader, more political, and social insights."'[38] Given such a state in the discipline of economics, which has continually occupied the central place in development studies, Hirschman rationalised his propensities, and intellectual needs, for 'trespassing' into other disciplines.

Hirschman felt that very early in its short history, development economics, which is a 'comparatively, young area of inquiry', began registering a 'decline'. That, according to him, was largely due to its own tunnel vision and limitation in perspective, generated by what he called 'monoeconomics'.[39]

The encounter of economic science with a complex area such as development, and the consequences of such an encounter, were not lost on a generation of its practitioners. For the first time in its march from strength to strength – and a strong analytical tradition which turned ideas into dominant paradigms – the discipline received a rude shock. The phenomena of development, it appeared, could only be sliced up artificially, to suit the intellectual approaches of the discipline. What was to be sliced up was something as complex as the development process itself, but the continuous outpouring of concepts and paradigms provided the discipline, making its incursions into development studies, with its own intellectual respectability, and thereby persuaded its practitioners to believe that the 'slice' that they were dealing with *was* the whole development process. Moreover, intellectual satisfaction was sought not in an ever-increasing depth of understanding of the problem but in the impressive series of deductions which followed the making of 'rational' assumptions.

Earlier, the Keynesian economics had tried to give a similar jolt to the purists in the discipline by interjecting the 'political' element into the picture. Later on, as awareness grew of social and cultural aspects of the development of various societies, the bulk of development economists made a concession, saying that since developing countries were a 'sui generis' group of economies they needed a special kind of approach in order to be understood. The special kind of treatment was rarely spelt out, and its very acknowledgement became a kind of a ritual, after which the development economists went about their business ignoring the 'sui generis' character of those societies.

To Hirschman, however, the acknowledging of the 'difference' and then going about one's business in a manner one was used to, was not good enough. He therefore repeatedly emphasised 'the need for trespassing' and 'criss-crossing' the traditional disciplinary boundaries.[40]

Hirschman also began to feel that the way social sciences had developed, by analytically abstracting phenomenon after phenomenon from the social reality, and never reversing the process to find the contexts from which phenomena were abstracted, had thus been largely responsible for the distorted way in which development studies were pursued. He therefore went back to seventeenth- and eighteenth-century themes and approaches, when segmentation between disciplines had not occurred. In his *The Passions and the Interests* (1977), Hirschman maintained, 'it seemed worthwhile to look back at their [seventeenth- and eighteenth-century economic and political actors'] thoughts and speculations, if only because of our own specialization-induced intellectual poverty' in the field of development studies.[41]

Subsequently, in his *Getting Ahead Collectively* (1984), Hirschman underlined the actualities of the development experiences of the countries of Latin America, which he maintained were at variance with the social realities of the industrialised countries and therefore required a different approach to them, both in analysis and policy. Consequently, Hirschman reminds us not only of the limitation of focussing on just one kind of development experience, namely the Western, but also of the lack of awareness of the fact that policies based on such an experience do not always produce the intended results elsewhere, and are sometimes even counterproductive.[42]

This then brings us to another major development economist, Bert Hoselitz, who made a significant contribution to the approaching of development phenomena from a wider perspective. He raised the question of distortions caused by the way in which economists analyse their data pertaining to non-Western societies. In his *Sociological Aspects of Economic Growth* (1960), Hoselitz critically viewed both theoretical tools and the way in which they are employed in the economic analysis of developing societies. In his words, '. . . western economic analysis is applied to cultures in which some of the values that are taken for granted in Occidental countries are either completely absent or are present only in strongly modified forms . . .'.[43]

For Hoselitz the body of economic thought which each of the industrialised countries has produced has much to do with its own social and historical conditions, and, as such, it cannot be extended to suit the economic experiences of different kinds of societies. Hoselitz illustrated his argument to drive home the point that some of the economic theories produced by one industrial country are not suitable even for another industrial country, let alone non-industrial societies.[44]

For him, economic theories based on pure economic values, during the time of Adam Smith and his successors – when 'constant relations between economic theory and economic policy were considered both necessary and obvious' – had their own rationale. But now we need to expand our theory of economic growth into 'a theory relating economic development to cultural change.'[45]

While it is too early to build a general theory based on such a shift, he thought, nevertheless we can begin to lay the groundwork for it by taking into account the movements of several traditional societies towards modernisation and with insights gained from such exercises, build a broader theory embracing economic development and cultural change. Such a theory would have the possibility of a much wider application than those based on notions of pure economic growth, and that too of only a few industrialised societies.

Hoselitz even wanted economic growth and cultural change to be viewed as integral parts of a wider 'social system' and felt that gradually enlarged boundaries of our theoretical knowledge would make increasingly important contributions to such a system. But before we reach that stage, much research needs to be done on the history and development of the actualities of the emerging societies.

In order to zero in on the social processes, which shape not only the economic order but social relations in general, Hoselitz began taking interest in theories relating to the social system, and in particular, in the theory of 'pattern-variables' as developed by Talcott Parsons.

There Hoselitz made a mistake. For the theories of Parsons were deeply rooted in the experiences of a few Western societies. His controversial conceptual tool of 'pattern-variables', instead of analysing the actualities of living societies and, in that process, refining itself, became a classificatory tool for extolling Western social and political conditions and disparaging those in non-Western societies. The injection of Parsonianism thus distracted Hoselitz from his pursuit of a broader, and inclusive, approach to development.

A generation of social science students were deeply attracted to the well-known journal which Hoselitz started, *Economic Development and Cultural Change*. However, given the powerful thrust of development economics, and the non-emergence of a new breed of development scholars with a broader outlook, the 'Cultural Change' aspect of the journal became less and less pronounced.[46]

Among other development economists who sought to look at development studies from a wider perspective, Amartya Sen began viewing economic growth along with equity, health and nutrition, and the condition of women. In his *Resources, Values and Development* (1984), Sen also touched upon social benefit cost analysis and ethical issues in income distribution as aspects of development in general.[47] Then there was Paul Streeten, who was deeply influenced by Gunnar Myrdal's approach. He developed, along with Javad Burki, the concept of 'the basic needs', which we discussed earlier.

Of all the branches of the social sciences, sociology, being the least committed to the exclusivity of its own area of specialisation, was in an ideal position to pioneer an integrative approach to various perspectives on development studies. In fact sociology owed its very birth to an intellectual opportunity, and challenge, to integrate various areas which fell within the broad and residual category of what could be called 'society'. Relatively older disciplines such as history, philosophy, political science, law and economics dealt with only specific aspects of 'society' with which their themes were related: the rest was left unexplored. It was sociology which then carved a discipline for itself out of the residual categories and also started making inroads into the older disciplines. In building such a jurisdiction for itself it had the basic experience of integration which no other discipline within the social sciences and humanities had, with the exception of philosophy. Sociology was, therefore, ideally suited for yet another round of cognitive exercise in integrating various perspectives on development studies. Together with the exercise of integrating such perspectives, it could have also moved into the various uncovered areas in development and, eventually, hammered out a sub-discipline by itself which could have become Development Studies, proper.

But as a discipline, sociology remained much too rooted in *Western* social experience, and the various concepts and theories which it developed also had the accretions of such experience. Consequently, a number of development scholars who were initially attracted to it, turned away when they discovered the deep West-centric biases in the body of theoretical knowledge which it formulated. What proved far more attractive, and useful, to development scholars was its closely related discipline, namely social anthropology.

As a discipline, sociology could not get out of the morass of the tradition–modernity controversy, to play a more effective role in development studies by integrating various perspectives on the subject. Barring Max Weber, few sociologists showed deep sensitivity to the basic difference between one society and another without reducing them to tradition–modernity or inferior–superior differentiation. But Weber's emphasis on the need to undertake a *nuanced* social and historical analysis of different societies fell on deaf ears. After him, differences between societies were seen, and interpreted, with reference to an all-round advancement of industrialised societies and an all-round backwardness of traditional societies.

Despite the fact that the social anthropologists did not go into development studies in a big way – most of them stopped at the broader notion of social change – they, more than any other specialists, were philosophically as well as intellectually equipped for it. Very early in the growth of their discipline, now over one hundred years old, they became aware of their own bias, not only in their perspectives but also in the theoretical tools which they used. The former – their awareness of a Western bias – protected them from making a naïve, even derogatory classification of the non-Western societies, and, instead, encouraged them to go in search of the essential social and cultural differences between societies. And the latter – their awareness of the distortive effect of the tools of knowledge – led them to enter a variety of deliberately sustained controversies concerning relativism–universalism, and then take a highly specific position of their own in that controversy. Their participation in such an ongoing controversy made them continually go in search of relative social truths. Since distortions occur all the time in the very act of knowing, the practitioners of the discipline often avoided macro areas where one's intellectual inferences begin to claim what is not always cognitively warranted. They even put a premium on discovering the actual, and, possibly the unique, and thereby avoided the intellectual fallacy of what I have called the *parallels and actuals*.[48]

The drawing of such narrow circles of inquiry, round their research problems, helped them to go, as it were, wherever their problem took them. The social anthropologists, in that sense, were little affected, in their specific problem-oriented approaches, by the segmentary approaches of other disciplines. They always examined the integral aspects of the problem that they were interested in and tried to become as inclusive as their own perspective and individual cognitive capacities permitted. They were therefore ideally suited to play an integrative role, albeit in micro areas, of development studies.

Only recently have social anthropologists started taking an interest in development studies. A number of international development organisations have also started making use of their background and skill. Nevertheless, in development studies as such they have yet to make their mark.

In the field of political science, very few scholars of Western origin have made attempts at integrating development perspectives or the part played, jointly, by social organisation, economic growth, and political development. One of the few exceptions to this was *No Easy Choice* (1976), by Samuel P. Huntington and Joan Nelson.[49] In that work the authors came to grips with the problem of the interrelationship, and integration in policy, of the three basic components of development, namely economic growth, social and economic equality, and public participation. They then went about exploring the nature of the sequences and imbalances which resulted because of the precedence of and emphasis on those components. The work assumed that at different stages, and during different historically opportune moments, developing societies can, and do, exercise their choice of accent of one over the other. Each choice, of precedence and relative accent, produces its own, not easily manageable and sometimes irreversible, consequences and imbalances. For instance, emphasis on political participation can slow down economic growth, and emphasis on economic growth itself may indefinitely delay an increasing measure of political participation. Similarly, an initial emphasis on social equality may slow down both economic development and political participation. Consequently, as the title of the book suggests, there are no easy choices for the developing countries to make.

IV THE DEVELOPMENT EXPATRIATES

Within political development studies, one of the least recognised contributions is the one made by scholars from developing countries, either resident or expatriate. Their contribution is still in its early stages. Since most of them are trained in Western universities, or even based there, they have taken some time to distance themselves from the various influences which have shaped their thinking and perspective on developing societies.

With the distancing came the unusual problem of having to work *outside* the mainstream of political development scholarship, putting at risk academic encouragement and support, publication facilities, and even appointments. But harder than that was the problem of crystallising their own perspective by critiquing the body of theoretical ideas which was developed largely to explain the social and historical experience of a few industrialised societies. Implicit in such a body of theoretical knowledge were the accretions of the time and place – seventeenth- to nineteenth-century Western Europe and North America – and yet, without much refinement, it was pushed to the status of a universally valid theoretical knowledge and then used to explain the emerging societies during the 1960s and 1970s. Only by critiquing such a received theoretical knowledge could the scholars from the emerging societies evolve their own distinctive perspective and position. But that did not sit well with the development academic establishment.

What the non-Western scholars thus faced in the process of academically distancing themselves from their Western colleagues was a twofold problem: of having to survive, academically, out in the cold, if they went against the mainstream and the establishment; and of having to put together, often hurriedly, a respectable theoretical critique to back up their distancing and repositioning. The indigenous scholars – barring those among them who wanted to stay on the international circuit of foreign visits, invitations to seminars and conferences, and collaborative researches and publications – had the home base to support them and give them the academic respectability of schools or approaches emanating from a specific developing country. But those who were expatriates had to pay a heavy price for their growing intellectual independence, in the form of frosty relationships, less than fair evaluation of their submissions for publication, and near-exclusion from the big research funds. But that has been the story of all expatriate groups, especially in North America: they survive, work hard, and eventually open up the access to opportunity.

Within political development studies, some of the earliest critics were the Latin American scholars who used the background of the international economic system, and the idiom of political economy, to express some of their highly original ideas. They forced, as we shall see in detail in Chapter 2, the political development scholars to think in terms of the actualities of the political development process of Latin American countries against the wider background of economic relations between nations. The various versions of dependency theory which have come out in the last two decades have raised some of the crucial questions which the earlier political development scholars had overlooked. As could be expected, those dependency theory scholars took a very long time to be heard as scholars worth listening to.

On their part, Latin American scholars, with their Latin (both Iberic and French) taste for theory, came out with some of the most fascinating works on authoritarianism, corporatism, and coups. This they did in order to establish the uniqueness of their historical and political experiences.

In all those works they went back to the nineteenth-century European tradition of explaining political development through political economy and political philosophy. The Latin American scholars, both indigenous and expatriate, thus went beyond the narrow confines of the sub-discipline of political development, in order to interpret their own historical and social experiences more effectively. More about this in Chapter 2.

Scholars from Asia, looking at political development in their own region, became increasingly disillusioned with Western political development studies, which took pure politics as the core issue. After an initial enchantment, they also became increasingly doubtful of the adequacy of the Western body of theoretical ideas in explaining some of the peculiar problems of their region.

Very early in their intellectual pursuits they came to the conclusion that in their part of the world, traditional social organisation, culture, religion and so on and the values implicit in them, played a far greater role in political development than was realised by the theorists of pure politics. And despite a pre-emptive scholarly output with a pure politics approach, dazzling scholars everywhere including in South Asia, the 1960s and 1970s saw some of the most painstaking empirical studies, leaning heavily on social anthropology, while trying to understand voting, party politics, leadership, decision-making, the democratic process and so on, against the background of culture, social organisation, religion, and economic factors. Such works, over the years, have become increasingly sophisticated in their methodology and theoretical argument.

Their different perception of the region, where they think that society, religion and culture are deeply enmeshed in the economic and political development process, helped them to distance themselves effectively from the pure political development theorists. And unlike Latin American scholars, with their emphasis on international political economy, the Asian scholars came out in their development studies with an emphasis on social and cultural anthropology. Such approaches were highly suited to the development peculiarities of their own regions. To such a growing diversity of approaches, some of the African scholars contributed yet another dimension. They wanted the students of political development to take into account the experiences of their societies, prior to the colonial intrusion, and what such an intrusion has meant to them as human beings in terms of racial, and economic and political development.

What we thus have in political development is a situation where the mainstream theoretical approaches have increasingly come into question. While the political development establishment hangs on to the purity approach, in different parts of the world scholars have been asking what other dimensions need to be added to the political so as to make it more meaningful and effective.

Expatriate scholars in sociology and anthropology have been equally critical of the tradition–modernity framework used in order to explain the complexity of social change in developing societies. Expatriate economists, who probably worked the longest within the mainstream intellectual tradition of economics, have begun to emphasise non-economic factors such as education, health, nutrition, and the status of women, as constituting integral aspects of economic development.

The development expatriates, as could be expected, spoke with many voices. What they nevertheless brought to bear on development studies was a first-hand knowledge of the complexity of their own societies. They thereby not only helped development studies by questioning the ethnocentric biases in them, but also enriched them with a variety of hitherto unexplored perspectives.

V   SOME GENERAL OBSERVATIONS

Let us now briefly examine some of the implications of the foregoing classifications, ideas and approaches in development studies. The more we probe into the interconnected aspects of the development process, the more we feel obliged to go deeper into such interconnections, interrelations, interactions, and the continua of various forces, in short, the entire development *Gestalt*, if such a term is permissible. Such an ambition must necessarily await not only the identification of empirically established interconnections between different aspects of development, but also the growth of a commensurate body of conceptual knowledge to help us undertake it. And in both those areas, empirical and conceptual, we can only make an incremental progress. There will, no doubt, be some leaps and quantum jumps with which the gifted scholars can favour us with but by and large such blessings will be fewer. What we need to do, therefore, is to go beyond our dissatisfaction with development segmentation, and initially build bridges between what is artificially chopped up until we discover the implicit internal relationships between various aspects and can do away with such bridges.

Moreover, it will be relatively less difficult to locate such integral relationships between different aspects in smaller and specific units of development inquiry at an empirical level, than at a wider societal and conceptual level. In such a case, our conceptual effort will be about something which has already registered itself empirically, and then further deepened in its perception, conceptually.

For that what we need, first of all, is a conviction that such an intellectual exercise is worthwhile for our improved knowledge of the development process. For what we have in front of us by way of development studies is a chopped-up development process – to suit the specialist demands of various disciplines – which was unchoppable in the first place. Looking back one wonders how on earth we could have chopped up, of all things, a *process*. And now we are required to pick up the pieces and put them together in a meaningful whole of interrelationships!

But besides such a conviction we also need a sensitive and probing mind which can traverse the development terrain, speculatively; and then we need to undertake pilot empirical studies, based on hunches and loosely constructed hypotheses; to be followed by conceptually oriented empirical frameworks with specifically defined hypotheses; and finally, conceptual inferences drawn from such an empirical groundwork to indicate the crucial areas of interconnections of components, their fruitful or inhibiting interactions with one another, and the nature of the continuum which they provide within the development processes of each instance under review.

The social science intellectual tradition is more in the direction of separating and slicing problems and issues for specialist treatment. As opposed to that, development studies are now making a counter-demand on our cognitive capacity. They want the social science analytical tradition, given to separation, slicing, and specialised analysis, to confine itself to the initial steps, and then to turn itself to the identification of the interconnection and morphology of the development process, to make itself meaningful in a broader, and in a relatively holistic, sense of the term.

In response to such a demand, disciplines like anthropology, sociology, and political science, which are traditionally given to incursions into other disciplines, will have, relatively speaking, a greater facility than economics, which is given to viewing itself as a complete discipline and carries forward such a self-perception even in development studies.

Much will then depend on our interest and ability to think in wider and more interconnected terms than our disciplines prepare us for. The ultimate advantage will be with the individual scholars rather than with the discipline. If scholars are so inclined, or so intellectually oriented, they will then be able to look at the development process more comprehensively.

Regardless of the future of a more inclusive approach to development studies, the disciplinary and segmented approaches, which serve their own purpose, are likely to continue unabated. This is because the very notion of scholarly excellence, and of science, is tied up with specialisation, and the knowing of more and more about the less and less. Thus the disciplines which have lived in isolation from one another, and developed their own independent 'scientific' character, are not going to give up what they are used to even when applied to development studies, the demands of which on our cognitive efforts, as we saw earlier, are different.

Much will also depend on the performance and lead which the scholars, who are dissatisfied with the segmented approaches to development studies, come up with. The onus is now on them to show that alternate approaches in development studies have a great many intellectual possibilities.

2 The Variety of Development Experiences

In order to venture into the complex terrain of development process and development theory, we need to cultivate a sensitivity to the variety of development experiences, on the one hand, and be able to forge the required conceptual tools to be able to interpret them, on the other. Our existing theories in various segments of development studies are, by and large, based on the development experiences of a handful of industrial societies of the West. They are also based on the assumption that, at least for the sake of theoretical discussion, you can engage in a drastic reductionist exercise so as to fit into a preconceived theory the complexity and plurality of the development experience. As long as a theory is plausible, seemingly logical, and even appealing, such an assumption implies, you can play down or even ignore whatever is not explained by it. By so doing you will have extended an area of intellectual construction, logical reasoning, and rationality, where so far chaotic and incomprehensible sense impressions have prevailed. There is no problem with this argument as long as such a cognitive exercise is treated only as a starting point.

But proponents of such an exercise, in the field of development studies, did not want to go beyond the initial speculative phase in theory construction. They did not want to face the challenges of the real world in which development occurred. What took the place of the exercise was a rival, and equally speculative, theory derived from some reigning models or paradigms in the disciplines. Cumulatively, such exercises resulted in stunting our sensitivity to the actual world of development experience and the different kinds of demands which it puts on our conceptual endeavours. There is then something to be learnt from those inadequate efforts. But unless we ask ourselves what went wrong, we are not likely to launch, increasingly, more adequate theoretical initiatives to explore the significance of the development experiences of the actual world.

For their theory construction in development studies, economists emphasised factors such as savings, capital, investment stimuli and so on; political scientists emphasised equality, participation, responsive public officials and political accountability; and sociologists emphasised modernity, specialised roles, and pluralism. We now need to put these in the perspective of the various locations, where, historically speaking, they made their first appearance. Together with that we need to identify the mix and sequence of the various economic, social and political factors which were involved in the development of different regions at different times.

For the purposes of theoretical explorations, we shall inject an element of pluralism into the discussion. In the past pluralism was often used in order to kill a theory which was riding high, by producing evidence of the simultaneous existence of something dissimilar. What we shall do, instead, is to start off with the fact of the plurality of development experiences and then explore the nature of the demand that such a position makes on our theory construction.

The chapter is divided into the following parts: (I) Western experiences of development and the variety of theoretical explanations, (II) Latin American development experiences and region-specific theoretical explanations, (III) Asian development experiences and unexplored and unattempted theoretical explanations, and (IV) some general observations. We shall now examine each of these in some detail.

I WESTERN DEVELOPMENT EXPERIENCE AND A VARIETY OF THEORETICAL EXPLANATIONS

When we examine the development experience of different regions, and within them of different countries, we are struck by its sheer variety. And despite our reductionist bias, diverse explanations have persisted side by side. The variety of development experiences, and theoretical constructs to explain them, when considered together, are enough to stimulate a pluralist perspective not only on development but on theoretical constructions too.

Unlike the *induced* development of the emerging countries of our time, the economic development of the countries of Western Europe has been a product of 'autonomous movements' within which a wide range of forces was involved. So very wide was the variety of such forces that Bert Hozelitz called the economic development of that region the product of the 'social forces' of a period preceding it.[1]

Similarly, Fernand Braudel, in his seminal work *Capitalism and*

Material Life: 1400–1800 (1967), argued that a countless number of forces, in the social and economic life of Western Europe, were involved before it was ushered into a materially more productive life which we call by the name of 'capitalism'. What also strikes the reader of Braudel's work is his listing of the countless earlier attempts to attain an economic breakthrough which did not materialise. Braudel has thus put an element of contingency, or chance, in place of the activist role attributed to a rising class by Marx and Moore. Within the framework of a chance convergence, Braudel examined the role of a number of factors which are not normally associated with economic development. He thus took into account the part played by population, daily bread, superfluity and sufficiency, clothes, fashions, power and metallurgy, technology, money, urban life and so on.[2] The social consequences of such diverse forces accidentally coalesced to produce new economic organisations which then crystallised into different forms of capitalism.

Finally, the greatest work in the field of social explanations of the development in Western Europe is arguably Max Weber's *The Protestant Ethic and the Spirit of Capitalism*, in which he traces the stimulus received by capitalism from a variety of Protestant denominations, including Calvinism, for its explosive development in the seventeenth and eighteenth century.[3]

In pre-capitalist Europe, particularly in Italy, the cities with flourishing international trade such as Venice, Genoa, and Florence, exerted an enormous influence on small states. Those cities built their own social structures and financial oligarchies in order to influence not only the state but the church as well.[4]

Such a clearly identifiable economic dimension became enmeshed with other factors, including religion, when the centre of European economic activity shifted from Italy to the Atlantic. Both in Holland and in Britain, the far-reaching consequences of religious movements affected the very orientation to economic action, and the growth of capitalism itself. In the above work, Weber sought to identify such an orientation.

In his work, Weber extensively dwelt on what he thought was the 'spirit of capitalism' without which its own ceaseless economic activity, increasingly rational organisation, and the significance of those two to the laws and politics of society, would not have been possible. For him, at least in the initial period, 'the spirit' of capitalism was ignited, and turned into an effective force, by factors which were not merely economic in nature. Along with the economic, religious factors had also played a part in building such a 'spirit'. But once built in its own effectiveness, it then did not require propping up by factors other than economic.[5]

In building his thesis on the 'spirit' of capitalism, and then going into the sources which made it possible, Weber became a subject of controversy in his own time and since. Nevertheless, his emphasis on the fact that other factors than economic go into the making of economic growth became an academically respectable exercise, especially with economic historians.

Weber, however, had much greater success in building a case for the essential plurality of economic growth under capitalisms of different kinds. That thesis appeared in its most effective form in his *General Economic History*. In that he maintained that different forms of economic production – such as the plantation economy, which depended on a servile class of workers, as in Latin America; the estate economy, which depended on stock raising as in Britain; and the share-croppers of Russia and Germany – constituted the matrices within which their subsequent economic organisations grew. Similarly, institutions such as guilds, which sought to regulate economic relations between craftsmen and their employers, have had far-reaching influences on the economic forms which emerged thereafter.

Then there was the shop production, with its own effect on the nature of subsequent forms of economic life. Various kinds of mills emerged, flour mills, water mills, saw mills, edible oil seeds processing mills, and soon, together with ovens, breweries, iron foundries, hammer mills, mills for preparing military weapons, and clothing – all these have had a far-reaching influence on the nature of economic growth in different societies. Then there was also the growth of mining of different kinds which contributed to the special kind of economic growth of those societies.

Facilities for commerce and banking, rational book-keeping, 'calculable' law, freedom of market, readiness to use technology for commercial purposes, free movement of labour, the lifting of barriers between internal and external economy, and the commercialisation of economic life in general, helped to build different kinds of capitalist modes of production in different societies of Western Europe.[6]

While emphasising the plurality of economic forms, Weber was always cautious, pointing out the complex diversity of their sources. In his case such a reference often went from the tangible to the intangible. In his words:

in the last resort the factor which produced capitalism is the rational permanent enterprise, rational accounting, rational technology, and rational law, but again not these alone. Necessary complementary factors were the rational spirit, the rationalisation of conduct of life in general, and a rationalistic economic ethic.[7]

In a sense Weber had moved away from the 'spirit' of capitalism, which took him to its religious roots in his earlier work, to the 'rationality' source of economic growth, in his final work.

Like Max Weber, R.H. Tawney too believed that there was much more to the economic growth of the countries of Western Europe than the economists were able to relate to or acknowledge. In his words:

> The Revolutions, at once religious, political and social, which heralded transition from the medieval to the modern world, were hardly less decisive for the economic character of the new civilization than for its ecclesiastical organization and religious doctrines. The economic categories of modern society have their roots in the economic expansion and social convulsions which accompanied the age of Renaissance and Reformation.[8]

Tawney thus argued that both the economic institutions and religious organisations of the countries of Western Europe registered profound changes in response to a number of social forces that were at work. Subsequently, changes in religious organisation radically altered the nature of the state and the quality of its laws, and thereby enabled the economic activity to be conducted in an increasingly secular manner, unburdened by the constraints of religion.

Such a transformation radically changed social and economic life in Western Europe. Countries like England and Holland, with their antecedent advantage over France and Germany – in the form of constitutional revolutions, powerful bourgeois bankers, shipowners, merchants and so on – moved with greater swiftness to exploit new economic opportunities. Such an advantage further speeded up 'the secularization of social and economic philosophy.'[9]

Tawney then goes on to document how the various strands of Calvinism influenced the individual's perspective on economic activity in general and thereby helped the nascent capitalism to become a full-blown economic system with its own economic, religious and political rationale to support itself. Capitalism thus had the direct as well as indirect support of a large number of non-economic factors.

Tawney's argument ran parallel to Weber's and was most useful to the latter when he was attacked by Troeltsch, Holl, Luthey, and Trevor-Roper. These scholars had challenged the causal relationship which Weber had implicitly assumed between the changes in religion and society, on the one hand, and economy, on the other. Troeltsch had criticised Weber for viewing Calvinism as a totalistic force altering all compartments of social life. And Trevor-Roper spoke of 'the stresses' exerted by Calvinism on the then social and economic organisation rather than directly altering it.[10]

Tawney's support for Weber, nevertheless, remained firm. He even extended his position to maintain that what happened under Calvinism, and its defence of economic interest, was nothing short of the 'canonization of the economic virtues'.[11] Tawney was joined by Momsen in arguing that no one could deny the profound social change brought about by Calvinism precisely at the time when capitalism was trying to assert itself.[12]

Weber's work raised many questions. After him scholars began to ask whether the transformation of Western Europe to 'this-worldliness' was the doing of Calvinism? Furthermore, did it actually trigger off 'individual activism'? Finally, which segment of society, in particular, came under its influence? Was it the segment which Tawney himself had identified, which was denied access to education, professions, and higher social status? Did such a description fit the Huguenots whose diaspora had brought them to Britain and Holland, where their own marginality had made them hardworking, enterprising, risk-taking and, therefore, ideally suited for capitalism? This description also suited the Jews, and from that Werner Sombart had concluded that 'the Jews were the true creators of Capitalism'.[13] Apart from Huguenots or Jews, the additional question was whether one could also identify similar groups of marginal people who had a comparable social and economic background to be able to register such a mobility. This last question led to a spate of research in non-Western societies trying to find parallels between their economically rising groups and those in Western Europe in the seventeenth to nineteenth century.

Various attempts at social explanations of economic growth, especially in non-Western societies, were often perceived, and conceptually analysed, in terms that were parallel to what had happened in Europe. Such attempts neglected, barring those which were carefully undertaken by economic historians and social anthropologists, the uniqueness of different social and historical situations in different societies, giving rise to economic growth of a different kind. But more about that in the section on the Asian development experience.

Let us now briefly take into account the economic and political explanations of the development process of the industrialised countries of the West. Such explanations often try to bypass the question of the 'source' of economic and political dynamism, especially in seventeenth-century Western Europe, for the simple reason that the search for it may lead to a process of infinite regress in economic and political history. What scholars often do is to identify, instead, some of the more powerful movements with recorded social consequences, and treat them as the starting point in their chain of arguments. With such starting points they then move on to various changes in economic and political organisation which either accompanied them or followed them.

In economic explanation, particularly, the idea is to arrive, as soon as possible, at a major development such as capitalism, which made all the difference to the economic growth and political fortunes of the Western world *vis-à-vis* the rest. Major political economists such as Marx, Moore and Schweinitz spent most of their scholarly life studying capitalism, and much less time on the period which preceded it. For them capitalism became the source of the economic and political development of Western Europe.

There is yet another interesting feature of the explanation of economic growth. Despite the process of individuation in Western Europe, as launched by Protestantism, justified by Lockean political liberalism, and carried into economic pursuits by entrepreneurial capitalism, the economic and political explanations of the development process were largely expressed through the idiom of class rather than the individual. Accordingly, social movements, migrations, guilds, commerce, banking, urban living, work in commercial and industrial undertakings, were all viewed as activities of classes. While the individual remained very much in the centre of political rights that were claimed or economic initiatives that were launched, he was, nevertheless, considered to be an expression or a voice of his class. The individual was thus considered to have only one identity: that of the class to which he belonged. In terms of social and economic reality, such an argument implied, one could not think of an individual outside his/her class.

Such a class idiom was carried by Marx right across European economic and political history, from the Greco-Roman period, through medieval feudalism, to the modern bourgeois society. Through the class idiom he also tried to illustrate the laws of social and economic transformation. Through the idiom of class, also, he was able to develop his theory of dialectical relationship between the productive and non-productive classes in various modes of economic production and their transformation. The slaves as opposed to freemen in the Greco-Roman period, serfs as opposed to landed gentry in the feudal period, and the proletariat as opposed to the bourgeoisie in capitalism, have been, in different periods, the main classes in various transformations in the social and economic organisation of Western Europe. For Marx, in particular, the dialectical relationship between the classes was not only an idiom of explanation of social and economic development but also a means of seeking social justice by fundamentally altering such a relationship itself.

The other two major thinkers in that genre were Karl de Schweinitz and Barrington Moore Jr. In his *Industrialization and Democracy: Economic Necessities and Political Possibilities* (1964), Schweinitz argued that the Industrial Revolution so rapidly accelerated the rate of economic growth that the social change generated by it could not be 'accommodated within the oligarchic political institutions bequeathed to Britain by the Glorious Revolution'. Such institutions, therefore, had to change and give way to the more participatory institutions within which the claims of the new urban middle class, and the working class, could be accommodated. To Schweinitz, therefore, democracy and industrialisation, at least in the Western world, were 'intimately, even causally' related.[14]

Some countries such as Britain, and the US to a lesser extent, were able to accommodate the particular demands of the new classes in their political institutions. France, among the early industrialising countries took longer. Even the unwilling German Hohenzollerns tried to make a feeble attempt to accommodate the demands of their new urban class.

But Schweinitz also believed that what happened in Western Europe and North America, whereby economic and political institutions changed simultaneously, was 'a function of an unusual configuration of historical circumstances which cannot be repeated. The Euro-American route to democracy is closed. Other means now must be devised for building new democratic states.'[15]

A similar argument was put forward by Moore, as we saw earlier, suggesting that economic forces reshaped political institutions, though not always in the direction of political liberalism. The landed upper class and peasantry, either together or separately, engaged in a thrust towards economic modernisation. Wherever there was co-operation between those two classes, as in Britain, the US, and France to some extent, the result was liberal democracy; when the thrust towards modernisation came only from the top, the result was fascism as in the case of Germany and Japan; and when such a thrust came only from the bottom, the result was communism, as in the case of Russia and China. To such a model, Moore admitted, India, with its tenth largest industrialised economy in the world, and liberal democracy, was an exception, and had followed a very different course.[16]

II LATIN AMERICAN DEVELOPMENT EXPERIENCE AND REGION SPECIFIC THEORETICAL EXPLANATIONS

Radically different from the development experiences of the countries of Western Europe, and the various scholarly perceptions and explanations which they have generated, are the experiences and observations of the Latin American scholars. Some of those scholars, in the latter category with a taste for conceptual analysis, have come out with astute observations of the fundamental difference in their development experiences from those of the Western countries. These have been expressed in various theoretical versions of economic dependency, political authoritarianism, and social corporatism. Most of their theoretical observations are cast within the reworked tradition of political economy rather than social and political anthropology. In fact such theoretical observations played down the element of culture altogether until they began to meet with resistance from scholars from East Africa and the Caribbean, where such theories were extended. In this section we shall analyse some of these Latin American perspectives on development.

The beginnings of the dependency theory, a fact which is commonly forgotten, are to be found in the writings of Dadabhoy Naoroji, the freedom fighter in colonial India. As early as 1866, he had argued in detail that India's agricultural and commercial resources were being drained away, systematically, to build the industrial economy of Britain. Such an explanation was dubbed 'the drain theory'.[17]

Since India then was the colony of Britain, such a disadvantageous relationship within the colonial context was taken for granted. But when the phenomenon of 'drain' was identified within a free-market situation, especially in the relationship between the countries of Latin America and the industrialised West, especially the United States, it immediately became a political and emotional issue.

In 1946, Raul Prebisch and his associates produced a report for the Economic Commission For Latin America (ECLA), in which they argued that the unequal relationship between the developed and developing countries was resulting in a continuous disadvantage, in international trade, for the latter.[18]

The report electrified a generation of Latin American scholars, both on the continent and abroad. Some of those scholars wanted to delve deeper into the very structure of international economic relationships which condemned their countries to such a disadvantageous position. In a number of Latin American countries such as Brazil, Mexico, Argentina, Venezuela and Chile, scholars simultaneously began exploring the notion of 'dependency' which resulted from efforts ostensibly meant for the 'development' of their respective countries. But what began to grip the minds of those scholars was the concept of 'dependency' itself. If it could be fully developed, those scholars began to feel, it would have within it all the necessary ingredients of a *paradigm*. As a paradigm it could then give them a new perspective on national and international relations, and identify exciting problems for scholars to research, enabling a return to the Latin American intellectual tradition, inherited from Europe, of expressing ideas through the idiom of political economy.

Since the Latin American economic conditions were seen as the direct result of the capitalist intrusions in their societies, one of the problems was how to accommodate Marxist theories of capitalism and imperialism within the emerging framework of dependency theory. The end result of this intellectual endeavour was that different scholars subscribed to the different aspects of Marxism, with very few of them escaping the wrath of Marxian purists for having mixed up a foreign element, such as dependency, in the revered corpus of Marxian theory.

While the thinking of the leading Latin American scholars, on dependency theory, was still shaping itself, there appeared a highly influential book by a Cambridge economist, Paul Baran, who argued in *The Political Economy of Growth* (1957) that the British actively underdeveloped India.[19]

What Baran thus interjected into the discussion was the phenomenon of deliberate 'underdevelopment', and he thereby created the need to know 'the morphology of backwardness'. The state of underdevelopment now could not be considered to have arisen because of a simple lack of effort towards development, but was arguably the result of specifically designed policies for those societies whose growth and development was likely to hurt, in the long run, the interests of the economically powerful countries. Subsequently, Andre Gunder Frank made that issue the central theme in his much discussed work 'The Development of Underdevelopment'.[20]

A number of Latin American scholars produced their ideas on the dependency theory by critiquing both the report of ECLA and modernisation theories produced by American scholars in 1960s. Among them Dos Santos and Cels Furtado in Brazil, Sunkel in Chile, and Cordoso and Faletto in Argentina, were the most prominent. Since the ideas of Cordoso and Faletto constituted the core argument of the dependency theory, let us analyse them in some detail.

In their *Dependency and Development in Latin America* (1979), Cordoso and Faletto sought to develop a kind of broad perspective on the dependency theory by taking into account interrelated social, political, and economic aspects of development in Latin America. But in formulating such an approach they wanted to work within the intellectual tradition of political economy rather than assign a dimension to socio-cultural relations.[21]

In order to present their arguments, concerning an integral relationship between external and internal politico-economic factors, Cordoso and Faletto adopted a structural approach. Since Latin American societies 'have been built as a consequence of the expansion of European and American capitalism,' we need to take that fact, according to the authors, as the starting point of analysis.[22]

Then there is the structure of internal socio-political relationships in Latin-American societies, which needs to be identified. The authors believed that despite 'coincidences of interests between local dominant classes and international ones',[23] it would be naïve to assume that the former are the mirror image of the latter. It would be equally fallacious to assume that the 'national socio-political situation is mechanically conditioned by external dominance.'[24] Moreover, the internal structure of relationships is under stress for change all the time. Thus by not subscribing to the extreme position of the early dependency theorists, whereby any and every local problem was attributed to the relationship between countries, the authors sought to undertake a much more discriminating analysis of the linkage of interests, internal and external.

In the 1970s, the dependency school became most popular on the campuses, and among younger scholars, for its ability to explain why the developing countries were not doing as well as they were expected to. Moreover, the theory conveniently shifted the blame from explicit colonial domination to subtle international business relationships, thereby sparing a generation of scholars the intellectual effort of getting down to the actuals of international economic relationships. At the height of its popularity, support or opposition to the theory was tantamount to being either for or against the international poor.

After the theory had held enormous sway on the campuses for nearly a decade, dissensions began to develop among dependency scholars themselves. One of the sub-themes of the dependency theory was that of centre–periphery relative advantages, whereby the more industrialised and former colonial powers were seen as the centres of new development, and prospering, and those surrounding them, that is the developing countries, were seen as dwindling. Curiously enough, there also appeared a parallel in the relationship between the scholars from the developed and developing countries, including those subscribing to the dependency theory itself. Accordingly, the dependency scholars who came from the United States, began to get much more credit for the new paradigm, even when their own contribution to it was insubstantial, than those from the developing countries, in particular Latin America, who had produced works of great scholarship.

Outside Latin America the only scholar known in the field of dependency theory was Andre Gunder Frank. Frank, according to Latin American scholars, produced the least number of ideas on dependency but monopolised all the adulation and limelight related to it. A generation of young American scholars, stifled by the classical and neo-classical theories of economic growth, the structural–functional approach in political development, and theories of modernisation as propounded by sociologists, rushed to embrace the dependency theory and its populariser in the US, namely Gunder Frank. Frank, in this case being in the centre, the US, and the Latin American scholars, being on the periphery, reillustrated the centre–periphery thesis in the scholarly domain.

On the American campuses, one rarely heard the name of Raul Prebisch who was the father of the theory. Moreover, the American scholars, influenced by the reductionist approaches of the popular-isers, did not want to probe deeper into the nuances of dependency theory which appeared in the writings of Latin American scholars.

Apart from the internal dissensions, dependency theorists were not looked upon kindly by the Marxist fundamentalists. For them the former were simply vulgarising Marxian class analysis and the theories of imperialism of Marx and Lenin.[25]

But the greatest blow to the dependency theory came from those scholars who had supported it in the past but had become increasingly sceptical of it. Such scholars thought that it was too stagnant, too devoid of actual realities of developing societies, and 'too economistic'.[26]

Outside Latin America, the reception to the ideas of dependency was varied. After an initial enchantment, scholars from the Caribbean countries began to feel that what they needed first of all was 'an adequate basis of local knowledge', with which to suitably refine and adapt imported theories. Some of them began emphasising the need to know more about the cultural values of the people before we theorise about them. Others emphasised 'collectivism and creativity', 'self-reliance' and other qualities within the Caribbean cultural tradition going back to African origin in religious movement (Rastafari) and music (Reggae). That in turn generated greater interest in how those traditions developed in Africa.[27]

So far as Asian scholars were concerned, the dependency theory had limited interest and acceptance. This was despite the fact that both Dadabhai Naoroji's 'drain theory' and Paul Baran's 'theory of underdevelopment' had India as their main illustration. The reasons for such a limited reception were threefold. First, India has had more than four decades of planned development experience since her independence. The resources for such a development have been increasingly generated internally. India now claims that for her Eighth Five-Year Plan, spread over the decade of 1990s, she will be able to generate the bulk of her required resources internally. In her case, the slow development is seen as a problem in rigid planned development, corruption, and an extraordinarily obstructionist bureaucracy. Then there is the problem of public accountability, which people in office have so far successfully dodged. The bulk of Indian scholars thus do not see the industrial powers of the West cheating them on a massive scale, though there are no doubt problems of getting better returns on raw materials and various other trade restrictions they have to face. Second, Indian scholars feel that the dependency theory also introduces an element of scapegoating which is likely to make the countries concerned even less involved in seeking improvement in the performance of various indigenous development agencies.

Third, there is the increasing realisation of the thick layer of culture affecting all aspects of India's development effort. Against such a background, the dependency theory is seen as yet another foreign import based on the social and historical realities of another continent. Moreover, its neglect of the cultural problems of the region where it first developed, namely the countries of Latin America, is seen as a serious shortcoming.

In recent years the 'four dragons' of Asia, namely South Korea, Taiwan, Hong Kong and Singapore, are widely considered to be illustrations of initial dependency turned into an aggressive competitive capability. The initial investment by the Western powers, as well as Japan, in the economies of those countries was motivated by profit and the expectation of continued dependence for further investment on the part of the dragons. But in less than a quarter of a century the situation was turned the other way round. The dragons, in particular Taiwan, have not only become a powerful competitor in their export of manufactured goods but have also started investing heavily in Western economies themselves.

Despite such shortcomings, the dependency theorists generated enormous intellectual excitement not only in Latin American countries but throughout the academic world. They brought to bear a unique dimension of their own *regional* development experience, on fresh explorations in development theory. After them it will be difficult for any serious scholar to go back to simplistic neo-classical or Marxist theories of development and ignore the perspectives generated by dependency theorists for the political societies of Latin America. Nor would it be correct to assume that the scholars who generated so much intellectual excitement in development studies in Latin America in the 1970s would totally disappear from the scene just because the initial round of their explorations in development theory stopped short of making their ideas acceptable to the wider community of scholars.

Let us now take into account some of the perspectives generated by the Latin American scholars on political development. Economic, military, and political institutions of Latin American countries have been a matter of puzzle for the students of political development. In recent years a number of Latin American scholars have sought to explain this by means of their lively, and theoretically rich, writings.

Those scholars tend to disagree with the Anglo-Saxon broad-stroke characterisation of most of the Latin American political societies as 'authoritarian' in the Western sense of the term. Latin American scholars also claim that in order to do justice to the actual character of authority in their political societies, we shall have to look carefully into the nature of their political heritage and the peculiar orientation of their legal and political institutions. At the centre of such a heritage lie the peculiar state-society relations, cast in the Iberic-Latin tradition, which ought not to be ignored.[28]

To begin with, there is the widespread permeation of the centralist tradition in most countries of Latin America. This is due, largely, to what have been characterised as the *four absences* in Latin American societies: the absence of feudal experience, absence of religious non-conformity, absence of a specific period of industrial revolution, and absence of the ideological currents associated with the French Revolution.[29]

Then there is the peculiarly urban character of most Latin American societies, which, together with the shock-absorbing role of bureaucracy, has often insulated those societies from the periodic tremors of political coups. So great has been the society-insulating capacity of the Latin American bureaucracy that the frequent coups are reduced to something which affects the very top few and not society as a whole. None of the coups are allowed to do to societies what the French or the Russian Revolution did. Such an insulation, however, also prevents those societies from acquiring their own periodic, cataclysmic, internal regeneration.

At the level of society itself, business is transacted by means of groups, with their base in classes, professions, interest associations, or the army. At the top of such groups emerge the wheeling and dealing élites who develop the necessary skill in transacting group business, to protect and enhance their interests in a constantly shifting political scene.

Such a background prepares the political societies of Latin America for what a perceptive scholar called *corporatism*.[30] Smaller groups find their place in, and are affiliated to, bigger groups, and the bigger groups, at the apex, become parts of big corporations, anchored in economic interests, military, political party, church or professional groups. Political society in Latin America thus becomes an arena for the interplay of vast corporations. Effective political business, the shaping of public policy, and so on, are brought about through the interplay and the relative strength of vast corporations.

Since the army, rather than the party or the union, is the most disciplined of the corporations, speaking with a single voice most of the time, it brings to bear, apart from the strength of its armour, the greatest effectiveness in its dealing with other corporations.

Moreover, as the Latin American scholars argue, the role of *the state* in their society is not fully appreciated by their Anglo-Saxon counterparts, who through representative institutions, and emphasis on individual rights, often take society far more seriously. Such a pro-society bias, they argue, is also to be found in the theories formulated by the social sciences which have primarily developed in the West. As opposed to that, in Latin American countries there has been an uninterrupted tradition of what has been called 'the dynamic and the visible role of the state'.[31]

As is evident from what we have briefly examined in this section, the development perspectives of Latin American scholars, based on their own experiences and perceptions, are materially different from those of the Western scholars, based on the experiences of the societies of the West. And the perceptions of the former no matter how diverse, come to acquire great significance in efforts to understand the development process of their region. In any attempt at theory construction, therefore, the peculiarities of the regional experiences and perceptions ought not to be overlooked.

III ASIAN DEVELOPMENT EXPERIENCE AND UNEXPLORED THEORETICAL EXPLANATIONS

The experiences and perspectives on development of the non-Western societies, in particular of Asia, are materially different from those examined in the two earlier sections of this chapter. Such experiences and perspectives, as we shall see in this section, are influenced and shaped by historical, social and cultural forces. Consequently, to do justice to the peculiarities of the development experiences of Asian societies, we need to consider, or reconsider, the phenomena of economic growth, political development, and social change within the framework of those societies' own historical and cultural experiences. Political scientists, anthropologists and sociologists are unanimous in their opinion that there is a thick overlay of culture on the political societies of Asian countries. And while the economists formally acknowledge such a position, the nature of their theoretical knowledge, which is almost entirely based in the development experiences of a few Western societies, prevents them from coming to terms with this vital fact.

To illustrate this contention, we shall consider in this section the development experiences of Japan, China and India. In that connection we shall also take into account the manner in which their own scholars view their development experiences. Since the development experience of India, especially at the grassroots level, is dealt with in detail in Chapter 3, in this chapter we shall only briefly refer to it, for the sake of comparison.

In recent years, Japan's phenomenal economic growth, and the social conditions which gave rise to it, have been a subject of much interest in the countries of the industrialised West. Nevertheless, the bulk of scholarly writings on it, despite protests from Japanese scholars, have sought to segment themselves on strict disciplinary lines. In this section, therefore, we shall focus on the broader background of the development experiences of Japan, and the manner in which her own scholars view them, so as to pin-point the new intellectual imperatives that they generate for a possible fresh round in theory construction.

In her seminal work, *Japanese Society* (1970), Chie Nakane, a leading Japanese anthropologist, argued as follows: 'in my view, the traditional social structure of a complex society, such as Japan, China or India, seems to persist and endure in spite of great modern changes.'[32]

Nakane emphatically rejected the view that further industrialisation of Japan would make her social organisation similar to that which exists in the countries of the Western world. On the contrary, the persistence of Japan's deeply institutionalised cultural values, and social peculiarities, which together have given to the Japanese brand of industrialisation a special character of its own, are likely to persist. It is such a relationship, between what is peculiarly Japanese in a social and cultural sense, and the nature of her industrial organisation and corporate life in general, which makes Japan a highly distinctive industrial society. What we need to identify, then, is how her changing social organisation, in its own peculiar way, has also become an effective part of her economic growth and political development

For Nakane, in that respect Japan was not alone. In her words: 'In Japan, India, China and elsewhere rich and well-integrated economic and social development occurred during the pre-modern period, comparable to the post-feudal era in European history, and helped create a unique institutionalization of social ideal.'[33]

Such an institutionalisation was not swept away by the advent of Western-style industrialisation, education, institutions and so on. As a matter of fact, it adapted itself to what came from outside. At the same time, it materially altered the character of what was emulated. Consequently, the curious blend of the Asian (different in different societies within Asia), created, structurally, different situations.

Those three societies of Asia, Japan, China, and India, were culturally and socially different from each other to begin with. On top of that there were differences in what was selectively borrowed, and the way it was borrowed, from the West. Finally, there was the wide range of interactions, in those societies, between the indigenous and the borrowed. Thus even during the ascendency of Western powers in Asia, a period marked by large-scale emulation of Western institutions, these societies were registering social situations which were vastly different from one another.

Structurally speaking, in Japan, compared to China or India, kinship figures much less prominently outside the household.[34] What then takes the place of kinship, incredible as it may sound, is one's place of work. The place of work thus provides a network of reciprocal relationships. One is thus *relating* oneself to others, in the place of one's work, by means of artificially forged ties, which in China and in India exist only within one's kinship structures.

For Nakane, therefore, the relationship between the employer and the employee goes much beyond contractual terms, unlike in the Western countries.[35] The employer in Japan becomes head of the family, as it were, and between him and his employee are created bonds of mutual obligation. What thus characterises Japanese social organisation, corporations, industries and so on is the phenomenon of loyalty and reciprocity which runs both ways. Given the notion of mutual obligation in the place of one's work and society generally, the question then is whether there is an all-pervading sense of fairness in Japanese society or not. Both Michio Morishima and Ron Dore, as we shall see later on, believe that there is.

Impressive economic growth often leads to questions concerning radical change in the normative structure of society. Max Weber, and other scholars, as we saw in Chapter 1, attributed economic growth under capitalism in the countries of the West, to the work ethic and the sanctification by Calvinism of profit as the fruit of one's labour. It has been asked, therefore, whether Japan's phenomenal growth since the Second World War was also a product of a corresponding change in her system of values. One of the major Japanese scholars who took up the challenge of identifying such a change in her history and culture was Michio Morishima. In his widely discussed work, *Why has Japan 'Succeeded'?: Western Technology and Japanese Ethos* (1982), Morishima tried to identify a religious source of her economic growth, just as Max Weber had done in his *Protestant Ethic and the Spirit of Capitalism*.

Morishima argued that the Japanese ethos was shaped over a long period of time, and not just decades before the outburst of her economic growth. For 'economic structures and economic relations are strongly conditioned by the national ethos'.[36] He, however, had to face the central puzzle that, unlike Calvinism's activist ethic of doing all that was necessary to one's environment to improve one's material life, Confucianism (it was assumed) had underscored the need for coming to terms with it no matter how very intolerable it was.

Morishima began by questioning such a rendering of Confucianism in relation to Japan. He maintained that the brand of Confucianism which was introduced there was different. Moreover, Taoism – which was later on transformed into Shintoism – was introduced into Japan about the same time as Confucianism. Taoism did not prepare society for either passivity or 'benevolence'. On the contrary, an activist element was very much in evidence in it. Such an element, coupled with the emphasis on education and social mobility during the Meiji era, transformed the very foundation of Japanese society. But there was one vital difference: what was emphasised, and appreciated, was the group's, and not the individual's, effort towards economic development and social mobility.[37]

For Morishima, therefore, what the Japanese acquired from their two major religions, Confucianism and Taoism turned into Shintoism, was 'an ideological driving force for solving problems which their society had confronted.'[38] Under these circumstances, the Japanese emphasised Shinto at a time of crisis and Confucianism in a post-crisis period.

What the two religions gave the Japanese was unique, and so, above all, was the manner in which their heritage was used in building and operating the social organisation. The social organisation acted as a cushion for experimenting with new forms of economic institutions until those suitable to the values implicit in it could be improvised and evolved. In that sense the Japanese industrial capitalism – borrowed from outside but improvised to suit the basic normative structure of her social organisation – produced economic institutions and practices which had no parallel in the Western societies where it had originated. Instead of competing individuals, Japan came to have competing corporations. So far as the individual was concerned, he entered, in his place of work, into another network of mutual relationships and obligations corresponding to those which existed in his immediate family. The two belief systems, namely Confucianism and Taoism turned into Shintoism and the peculiar way in which they were adapted to meet new economic and social demands, thus provided an emphasis on hard work, discipline, pride in work, loyalty, compassion and togetherness.[39]

But Japan has not stopped at this windfall coming out of a highly effective use of her traditional normative structure. She has continually built on it by means of education and the sharing of information.

Japanese society, like its Indian and Chinese counterparts, is multilayered.[40] Within it, the different periods of her history, internal developments and external influences, have all become a complex of coexisting cultures which, in a subtle manner, continue to exercise influence on her people.[41] Consequently, their living significance to those societies would be lost if we studied them in terms of discrete historical periods or, as is often the case in viewing Japan, as either a 'borrower' or 'late-developer' society.

Japan also brought about one of the greatest revolutions known, in developing the skills of her people. Such a development, in turn, phenomenally enhanced the capacity of her people not only for economic growth but also for the continued development of their own skill. In the words of scholars who studied this development: 'ample evidence now exists demonstrating the economic contribution of formally organized schooling (presumably transmitted into new capacities, knowledge, and skills that are put to use in modern productive processes) to the growth of economies.'[42]

Thus along with the usual economic factors of capital formation, labour supply, structural change in the economy, monetary and fiscal management, consumption, savings, reinvestment, and effective penetration into international market, with the phenomenal growth in education, and together all these have made the necessary difference to the nature of Japan's development.

By the end of the First World War, Japan had attained close to 100 per cent literacy, whereas the US, despite her material and human resources, could barely reach 80 per cent literacy in the 1980s. For an inordinately long time, Japan, with her resolve to catch up with the societies of the West, called herself 'a learning society'.

Education, and the quality of it, helped Japan to convert economic and technological measures into socio-economic measures and vice versa. No matter what the new measures or policies were, the principal focus always has been on the human beings. Since they are the greatest resource, an ever-enhancing basic resource, public expenditure on their further development is never resisted. It is thus one of the few societies which invests in its own people and therefore ensures a continual growth of itself.

What has also helped Japan to aim at a broader conception of growth is her deeply internalised sense of social and economic fairness. Ronald Dore, in his *Taking Japan Seriously* (1987), has pointed out how frequently the theme of 'fairness' recurs in Japanese society. Whether one takes industrial training, the wage spectrum, authority in industry, incomes policy, or whatever, the underlying emphasis is on fairness.[43]

The all-pervasive notion of fairness in Japanese society, puts her in a favourable position *vis-à-vis* an unequal class society such as that of Britain, and a rigidly unequal caste society like that of India. Britain's economic growth, and a widening social inequality, needed a powerful labour movement and a continual expression of adversarial relation between labour and management, to enforce some degree of economic fairness. Similarly, in India, despite professions of 'socialism', and rigidly planned development since independence, the inequalities have not only widened, but the number of people below the poverty line has increased. Since there is much more to the poor in India than their mere economic deprivation, as we shall see in Chapter 3, there is as yet a limited understanding of the complex nature of her poverty.

All this suggests that the social scientists need to look again at the nature of society, in developing countries, so as to put various aspects of development in their proper perspective. The earlier round of research into their societies, especially in the 1950s and 1960s, was heavily influenced by theories which were deeply rooted in the social and historical experiences of a few Western societies. As opposed to that we now have increasing amounts of empirical data on society in developing countries and competing theoretical structures formulated by indigenous scholars. A fresh round of research, incorporating their findings, and then reformulating existing theoretical frameworks, could be of immense value to development studies.

The economic modernisation of Japan, at least in its earlier phase, was the product of the effort of the middle level *samurais*, who were not allowed to own land, rather than that of an entrepreneurial class, as was the case in Western countries. It was undertaken with a view to catch up with the societies that were already industrialised.

Such a thrust towards the economic modernisation of Japan, which was imposed from the top, had its own far-reaching effect on the nature of her society. The countries of the West took two to three centuries to bring about their industrialisation and simultaneously underwent a fundamental change in their social and political relationships and attitude to political authority. As we saw in the earlier section of this chapter, especially while examining the ideas of Karl de Schweinitz and Barrington Moore Jr, the forces of entrepreneurial capitalism also brought about the necessary difference to the oligarchic nature of the public institutions of Western Europe, and made them 'permissive' of what the new and risk-taking class of entrepreneurs wanted to do. Such a thrust thus reshaped the legal and political institutions and made them responsive to the pressure from the growing urban middle class and, later on, the working class, for an increasing measure of participation in decision-making. Consequently, industrial capitalism in the countries of Western Europe, by virtue of social change generated by its thrust towards economic modernisation, ended up by establishing liberal democracy in those societies.

That did not happen in Japan. While the Japanese society could emulate various industrial techniques and practices which were at the root of the industrialising economies of the West, what it could not emulate was the broader social change which had resulted in the societies in which industrialism had originated. Initially, therefore, the emulated economic and industrial institutions and practices functioned side by side with the indigenous, with their own sets of compartmentalised norms and rationalities, until such time as 'bridges' were built between the two, which finally led to a gradual emergence of what could be considered a unique product of the interaction of the two.

The uniqueness of the Japanese industrial society – distinguishing itself in terms of labour–management relations, attitude to work, and primary group type of relations on the shop floor – further distinguished itself by its enormous emphasis on education, information, the learning of the new skills, and, above all, building of human capacity to absorb the results of the ever-increasing technological innovations.

Socially speaking, Japan's industrialisation did not destroy her deeply ingrained associated living and mutual ties, but externalised them on the shop floor and offices, making them the incomparable instruments of collective efficiency and quality. That was then further reinforced by the pervasive sense of fairness, eliminating the adversarial conflicts which characterise industrial relations in the Western countries.

But the basic question remained as to how all these antecedent social features, which proved to be highly advantageous in building a new kind of industrial society, featured in the functioning of her liberal democracy. Western scholars such as Ruth Benedict, Ronald Dore, and Marion Levy faulted Japan for not being able to produce a process of individuation which (they assumed) must inevitably go with modern economic and political life. Since the countries of the West went through such a process, it was seen as a universal imperative before a society could qualify as 'modern'.

In his subsequent writings on Japan, however, Dore's emphasis on individuation, as a necessary qualification for being 'modern', changed. Along with Ezra Vogel, he began to see that the the group-submerged character of the individual of Japan was not necessarily a disadvantage in her economic life.[44]

The liberal political institutions of Japan, which were imposed on her by the Allied Occupation between 1945 and 1952, have yet to face the operational challenges, especially during lean economic years, of political élite divisiveness and political resentment generally. Since the establishment of her liberal institutions Japan has not faced those problems in their unsettling severity. So far the volume of voter turn-out too, out of 'duty', has been very impressive. But sooner or later there will be critical issues which will test the depth of commitment of her people to liberal values and institutions.

At the turn of the present century, Japan occupies a special position among the non-Western societies. She has, in certain respects, excelled Western countries in science, technology, and management of resources, thereby forcing the scholarly world in those countries to pay attention to what made that possible, not just in terms of 'correct' policies and institutions, but in broad social and human terms. And at an intellectual level, she has also forced the Western academia to enter into what Kinhide Mushakoji called an 'inter-paradigmatic dialogue', taking seriously the body of ideas other societies have produced so as to justify claims to universal validity.[45]

Let us now briefly examine the complexity of China's development experience and the crisis of political accountability and participation in 1989. Since the latter came as a surprise to most scholars, and since not much is known about the actual operation of the communist political system in rural or in urban China (excepting that some measure of economic liberalisation, led to a demand for a corresponding liberalisation in the political field which was brutally put down), we shall mainly confine ourselves to the historical evolution of the crisis against the background of China's own development experiences.

Even before the crisis of 1989, the scholarly writings on China had presented divergent views, falling in the broad categories of 'sinocentric' and 'ethnocentric'. The former rested on the claim that the Chinese society is far too complex for foreigners, always in a hurry to speak or publish, to understand, and the latter rested on Western views 'supported by universal statements'.[46] Moreover, China has also been a society subject to controversy relating not only to approaches but also to the range of themes and issues to be included in any examination of it.[47] As in the case of Indian society, scholars have never felt assured of the adequacy either of their scholarly efforts or of their conceptual resources to understand Chinese society. Each unexpected event in China, in the form of the Cultural Revolution, or limited experiments with the market economy, or the participatory crisis of 1989, brought home to scholars how much more they needed to know about her before they could confidently venture an opinion, let alone a judgment, on her performance. It might be, therefore, worth our while to have a second look at her development experience since the establishment of the communist regime.

By 1950, the Chinese Communist Party had gained control of mainland China, and built a powerful state to undertake far-reaching economic and social reforms in society. Its immediate task was to mobilise the people in rural and urban communities, to make education, including political education, available to a large number of people, to establish heavy industries, and, finally, to deal with recalcitrant elements.

In the earlier period, China was also trying to apply the 'Soviet' model of development to politics. Under these circumstances, the members of the party penetrated far and wide into rural and urban areas, undermined old hierarchies, built new economic organisations, and brought people of all ages into the schools for the new education.[48] That was then followed up by the introduction of land reforms, collectivisation, and communes.

Given the highly centralised leadership, together with deep and constant involvement in the mobilisation of people towards radical social and economic goals, the new regime in China not only lost a critical perspective on the actual results of its policy but also the possibility of a painless course correction at a later date. Whatever was introduced, therefore, was allowed to go on until the top leadership wanted it changed. Consequently, the policies of 'The Great Leap Forward' in 1958–60, and some of the supposed 'work miracles', remained mere rhetoric, incapable of being viewed in terms of results generated by them. The same was true of the Cultural Revolution. Once introduced, there was no mechanism either to evaluate it or even stop it. It had to be the policy as long as the people who introduced it were in power. It was only when Mao died, and his successors started floundering, that Chinese society could bring to bear criticism of the previous regime under the headlines of 'errors in economic guidelines', 'drawbacks of the managerial system', and so on.[49] Only the *past* leaders and regimes could be criticised. When the students in Tiananmen Square tried to criticise the contemporary regime, they were ruthlessly suppressed with the help of tanks and machine guns. Even in criticism the leadership had to give the lead.

By early 1980s, China had begun asking for international assistance. Its legal system was seen as offering very little security to individuals. Moreover, it curbed individual initiative and social dynamism. The harm done by the Cultural Revolution, and its attack on various professions, had created wide gaps in China's capability to look after her problems in specialised areas. It was then left to China's new programme of modernisation to find solutions to those problems.

The various efforts at select liberalisation and modernisation in the economy had quick results in terms of productivity as well as inflation. Agricultural and industrial growth in certain fields recorded impressive gains, but they also put in jeopardy the controlled price structure in various other items.

From a cast-iron state and its command economy, what the reforms introduced was 'competition among enterprises under socialist state ownership'. But such 'competition', as the Chinese scholars were at pains to describe it, was different from competition under capitalism.[50]

Such changes, nevertheless, were not without their own social and political consequences. The lower level leadership, and the intellectuals and students, took them to be a signal for increasing liberalisation and a retreat from Marxist-socialist positions and policies. But the top leadership had neither entertained such a fundamental shift in official position, nor was it able to send clear signals as to how far it was prepared to go. From time to time the leaders at the apex appeared to be engaged in finding solutions to specific problems without abrogating what had been painfully built, by way of a socialist society, over a period of four decades. Consequently, the top was quick to come out with the condemnation of what it called 'bourgeois liberalism' or 'ideological pollution', and asserted the superiority of the 'socialist spiritual civilization'.

In all this the most unenviable task was that of the party theoreticians and loyal academics, especially at the Institute of Marxism-Leninism and Mao Zedong Thought at Beijing. They were supposed to balance their earlier ideological commitment with what the leaders now wanted them to do. Within such a need for tightrope dancing, some of them also saw a genuine opportunity to do solid academic work on the question of what socialism can and should mean, within the context of the Chinese historical and social conditions. In that connection the various volumes which appeared from the Institute in 1984, 1985, and 1987 make interesting reading. Those volumes were at pains to explain the post-socialist phenomena of China which they claimed was going to be different from Western capitalism. They preferred to call it 'state capitalism' and exhorted their readers to understand the special nature of it. As Yu Guangyuan put it: 'the state capitalism now coming to the fore in China is a new phenomena in a new historical context, a phenomena vastly different in significance from that of the past.'[51]

Earlier, the Marxist scholar Su Shaozhi had maintained that Deng Xiaoping's assertion that there is a distinct need to build 'socialism with Chinese characteristics', had opened up a new world for the Chinese scholars. This is because such an emphasis gave much-needed legitimacy to research undertaken by those scholars who wanted to study Chinese communism against the background of 'history, culture, people, their habits and psychology as well as way of life.' It suggested that what they should concentrate on was 'what should be the distinguishing features of the economic structure, the political structure, the social relations, the cultural structure under socialism with Chinese characteristics.'[52]

The Chinese Marxist scholars were thus in the process of formulating their own perspective on the nature of their society and economy, which, along with Marxist ideology, could be derived from their own indigenous social and historical background.

But the events leading to 'the democracy movement', with its massive support from the students demonstrating in Tiananmen

Square in Beijing, in the summer of 1989, confronted academics with yet another challenge. Both Deng, and the academics supporting him, had overlooked the fact that with the increasing emphasis on pragmatism, modernisation, the opening up of the economy, and student exchange with Western universities, there was also going to be an increasing questioning of governmental unresponsiveness, highhandedness, favouring of kin, and corruption in general. It became clear that one could not prevent the questioning of performance, from economic matters to political issues. Moreover, after the revolution the Chinese rulers allowed 'criticism' only after the event. The question that the students, and the academics who joined them, asked was whether the right time for such criticism was not when the events themselves were in progress. Attracted by the appeal of 'freedom' in Western liberalism, and also in Marxism in its pristine purity, encouraged by the campus culture of the Western universities and the media, the Chinese students displayed a courage rare in human history. Despite the repression that came about, they prepared their society for yet another round of political change to follow.

Social and political change in China, since the revolution, has been a subject of much speculation and controversy. Apart from the extreme views of no change or total change, there has been the questioning of certain theoretical perspectives through which those changes are perceived. Such theoretical perspectives explain social and political change in Western societies rather than in the complex multilayered society of the Chinese.

Chinese society is one of the oldest in the world, with a baffling number of cultural layers. In each of those layers there has been an extraordinary range of philosophical activity, with an emphasis on values and ideas which have had an enormous influence on China's society, and on the conduct of her people generally. Some of those cultural layers, with a normative emphasis of their own, came from, among other sources, the teachings of Confucius, Buddhism, the School of Legalism, Taoism, Marxist-Maoism, and, finally, recent attempts at pragmatic modernism. Each of these layers left behind certain values, and a sense of social direction, which either integrated with the others or just stood by itself.

Mao was fully aware of the cultural background of Chinese society and, in particular, of the influence exerted on it by means of the values of Confucianism. And he was, therefore, constantly engaged in trying to uproot those values, albeit with little or no success. Since those values affected human relationships in general, Mao and his men sought to redesign institution after institution, so that those values might lose their hold on the people.

Such stubborn persistence of the cultural background, and the ineffective operations of the new institutions within it, made any fundamental change in Chinese society extremely difficult. The concentration of power dating back to the pre-Maoist period was easier to deal with than the reshaping of the network of social relationships, with their implicit norms of reciprocity, harmony, and attitude to authority in general. Mao, determined to change them, brought to bear the might of his government, party, and the army to make people conform to the new values and approaches which he and his men had introduced.[53]

Expatriate Chinese scholars, working in North American universities, emphasised the need to take the study of Chinese society seriously and consider against its background the operations of the Maoist economic and political institutions and the recent changes in them. In that connection their contributions to the volume *China's Heritage and Communist Political System* (1969)[54] constituted a watershed in Chinese studies. Earlier, Western scholars with much less access to Chinese, and an inclination to see parallels with Western social and political experiences, had put an enormous emphasis on an institutional approach. What the new generation of Chinese scholars did was to supplement that approach by identifying various processes of change, adjustment, and development.

One of the least explored areas within Chinese society is the kinship structure and its interaction with the new political system. Such a structure has survived, as in India, although not in Japan, through the ups and downs of recorded history. So strong is that structure, both in China and in India, that in actual social relationships, whether in the office, or on the shop floor, or in the professions, people create 'pseudo kinship' ties where none exist. They are inclined, even culturally compelled, to look at social relationships through the perspectives of kinship, real or artificially brought about. Such a background creates a special problem for a communist leadership which wants to regroup people round the goals of distributive justice to be attained through conflicts. For such a leadership, social goals decide the nature of relationship, and not the pre-existing social structures. Only intensive anthropological field research in Chinese rural communities, in future, will be able to tell us how much the traditional social relationships, and, in particular the kinship structure, have changed.

The contemporary Chinese political system is in a state of turmoil. In less than four decades it has been subject to four fundamental attempts at change: Maoist Revolution, the Cultural Revolution, modernising reforms, and mass upsurge for democratic reforms. And in the absence of careful research at all levels of society, particularly at the grassroots level, to determine the precise nature of the changes that have actually come about, we are left only with educated guesses. But such guesses have also repeatedly taught us, especially in recent years, that we need to know more about the social and cultural background of China, including the changes that have occurred in it, before we can talk about its development experience with some degree of certainty.

This then brings us to our examination of development perspectives on India. India, an open and democratic society – with a living heritage of a classical civilisation, which in parts wants to question and blend the modernising achievements of Western societies, with a large body of self-assured élites, well versed in the arts of self-expression – has produced a range of development perspectives which have few parallels. The development experience of India has been a matter of great interest, and concern, to a number of leading social scientists. With so much going for her – the cultural heritage, the commitment to liberal values, some of the greatest leaders of this century, vast and highly trained manpower, and enviable international interest and support – India should have done better in her development performance than she actually did. Her less than expected performance, therefore, has become a development puzzle and a matter of endless scapegoating.

The slow pace of economic growth in India has aroused its own controversy. Soon after independence she made an earnest attempt to become a planned democratic society, imbibing the best of Fabian socialism. While her democratic structure, despite a lot of onslaughts, has remained intact, her economic performance has remained unimpressive. What is worse, despite official claims to 'socialism', she has nearly doubled, since her independence, the number of people below the poverty line, and has thus emerged as one of the most uncaring societies in the world. And all this despite the fact that she had a lot of things going for her. In the words of a perceptive economist, India now possesses:

a well diversified resource base, a large domestic market, a reasonably stable political system, a relatively successful experience of national integration, an experienced bureaucracy, a large fund of entrepreneurial talent, the world's fourth largest pool of scientific and technological manpower ... a fairly elaborate industrial infrastructure, and in recent years a high saving rate and a large inflow of foreign exchange through remittances by Indian migrants abroad.[55]

For her limited development, the economists are inclined to blame the wily politicians and the vested interests. The politicians, in turn, blame the economists for their policy proposals which were derived from 'foreign' models, and their limited understanding of the complexity of Indian social conditions. Finally, the politicians also join the economists in blaming the bureaucrats for their obstructionist mentality, which is reminiscent of the colonial days.

In their account of industrialisation of India, economists fondly mention the fact that as late as the nineteenth century, India was not an importing country so far as manufactured metal goods were concerned: 'Except for an insignificant amount of luxury goods, like richly carved swords, and occasionally, canons, India imported *no* manufactured metal products before the nineteenth century. In foreign trade India was very much an exporter of manufactured products and an importer of primary or intermediate goods.'[56]

Not only that, as early as the seventeenth and eighteenth century, India produced a merchant class, with vessels of her own for international trade. Such a class was backed up by several trading caste groups in her different regions, conducting internal trade on the subcontinent on highly specialised lines. Both those groups of traders needed an elaborate system of financial facilities, book-keeping, and banking. A perceptive historian has given a glimpse of such an infrastructure of trade and commerce in Ahmedabad, one of the many Indian cities.[57]

The advent of the British – as traders first, then traders bartering cash and soldiers for land, then selectively financing Indian trade and industry to strengthen their own economic base at home – began to change the nature of the Indian economy. It began to serve as a support for the British traders, and this, coupled with the policy of revenue collection without responsibility towards agriculturists, radically altered it from a vibrant exporting economy to one that was barely able to fight the exploitation by revenue collectors and the incredible greed of their middlemen. Finally, it became chiefly an exporter of raw material.

The Indian effort at development, since independence, had to address itself not only to the economic setbacks received during colonial rule, particularly in the field of agriculture, but also had to edge upwards in industrial development and build the technological and managerial infrastructure needed to sustain and advance it. Then there was the vision, at least in the euphoric post-independence days, of reattaining the heights of her classical civilisation. But in a changed world, with at least two centuries of loss in normal development time, an exploding population, and deeply institutionalised social inequality, such a vision proved to be illusory. It even evoked a kind of self-criticism whereby India's élites believed that nothing was going right within their society. At times they became so obsessively self-critical, and so preoccupied with their traditional role of passing moral judgments, that they even forgot that each public criticism also increased their own responsibility to get involved in improving the social situation.

The leaders of the Indian nationalist movement, in particular Jawaharlal Nehru, who were deprived of the use of the apparatus of the state during the period of their subjection, decided to make full use of it after independence. And that is what they did, in a big way: Nehru opted for 'planned development', with the help of the Planning Commission, to mobilise the human and material resources of the country.

The achievements of planned development were not as impressive as was expected. The economists and politicians, as stated earlier, blamed each other for it. The growth rate, for a long time did not inch above 3.5 per cent, and the well-known economist Raj Krishna even dubbed it 'the Hindu growth rate'.

The planned development facilitated the rise of certain groups of people. Given the deeply institutionalised social inequality, the response to development stimuli was different among different social segments. While large blocks of people moved up into the category of the big-ticket-item buyers, purchasing scooters, cars, refrigerators, televisions, apartments and so on, close to one-third of the population, most of it in rural areas, sank below the poverty line during the four decades of planned development towards a 'socialist' society.

India came to have the unenviable distinction of being 'the largest single country contributor to the world's poor'.[58] Over the years various attempts have been made to 'solve' the problem of rural poverty, but due to 'leakages', 'non-utilization or mis-utilization' of funds, no appreciable difference was made to their condition. Even in regions where economic development registered a faster pace, the condition of the poor did not improve substantially.[59]

Indian economists also produced impressive literature on rural poverty. But almost all of it tends to abstract *poverty* from the poor, so as to be able, to use Amaratya Sen's expression, to identify and measure it.[60]

To make possible the collection of hard-nosed data on any particular aspect of economic phenomena, such an exercise in abstract analysis may be deemed necessary. But there is much more to the poor in India than their economic deprivation, and the question is how far those additional factors have been responsible, along with the economic factor, for the continued state of rural poverty.

Since the dawn of Indian civilisation, the poor have been from the lower castes, untouchables, and tribals. Consequently, there must have been some relationship between their position in the social hierarchy and their economic condition. Then there is the load of *karmic* rationale which prevents the poor from shifting the blame for their economic deprivation from the makers of us all, to those mortals who have more than their fair share. The poor in rural India talk about *Karma* much more than the better off. The question, once again, is whether there is a relationship between what they believe in and their economic condition. The bulk of the poor in rural India do not believe that the various professed rural development efforts are for them. They have so deeply internalised their own marginality to society that they are unable to avail themselves of what has been provided, formally, in public policy for them. They have thus crippled their political capacity to get from democratic India what is earmarked, year after year, for them. More about the problem of rural poverty in Chapter 3.

To such a many-sided problem, the poverty studies, with their one-dimensional, economic approach, do not do sufficient justice.[61] In recent years, there has been an increasing awareness on the part of the economists that they should take into account the non-economic factors while studying poverty. But they also feel that to include the cultural contexts of poverty, as do the anthropologists, would restrict or even inhibit 'wider generalization.'[62]

Within the field of economic growth, nevertheless, the controversy surrounding the suitability of various concepts in the discipline to the problem of the economic development of India, did not generate sufficient interest. In fact it rarely went beyond the level of polemics.

Expressing his dissatisfaction over the work done on 'employment' and 'unemployment', from the perspective of economic science, Gunnar Myrdal commented as follows: 'unfortunately, persons responsible for statistical enquiries in the region [India], and behind them the Western and indigenous economists and planners, have been reluctant to scrap received doctrine and to begin afresh by formulating a new conceptual kit appropriate to their economic conditions.'

But Myrdal, wrote Amartya Sen, met his match in P.C. Mahalanobis: 'steeped as he is in the concept of the West, Myrdal cannot help evaluating the history and events of South Asia within the framework of those concepts.'[63]

Needless to say, such polemics did not advance the questions of the adequacy of concepts which ignore the contextual background of economic problems. A full-scale debate on this question, among the economists, has yet to take place.

The Indian political society has been regarded as one of the most complex in the world. It has ruined the reputation of many a scholar who has been too naïve and simpleminded about it. Even the complexity of its development process has come as a major challenge to the corpus of theoretical knowledge in the field. A wiser, and sadder, British scholar once said that: 'One can write nothing of India without immediately perceiving that the reverse is also true.'[64]

To such a complex society, the theories of modernisation, with their limitations and ethnocentricity, do the greatest injustice. Not only have they failed to take into account the Indian syncretic capability, for accommodating the extraneous and the contrary, but they have also come out with the total rejection of her indigenous characteristics as 'traditional', and, therefore, backward.

Unlike the Western societies, where social and political institution have evolved, along with a broad acceptance of their normative structures, the Indian social history – due to perennial wars, conquests and the resultant periods of social destabilisation – has witnessed phases of glory and disaster. Each phase of relative calm had its own achievements and left behind its own cultural deposits. The net result of such a historical experience has been a baffling heterogeneity of social and cultural norms, values, perspectives, directions, most of which have some bearing on the private and public conduct of her people and on her political society in general.

Her chequered history, mind-boggling internal diversity, hetero-geneity of norms and values, and extraordinarily rich intellectual life, together, resulted in six major schools of philosophy, and the pursuit of abstract thought in various fields. These then helped Indians cultivate, and retain through the ages, a taste for intellectual reasoning and quality of human spirit. But only individuals *qua* individuals could pursue such values. Consequently, one of the by-products of her social history also has been an extreme degree of individualism built round the intellectual and spiritual pursuits of the individual.

Simultaneously, Indian social development took place in the other direction. The intellectual pursuits were for the élite who could cultivate their mind and spirit by means of learning. But so far as the bulk of the society was concerned, it was tied down to a rigidly hierarchical social organisation and was guided by the holy texts as interpreted by the holy men. Such a dichotomy of social development continued right through Indian history. The élites, unless they were socially concerned, left the bulk of the people to find their own sense of social direction, and devoted their life to the pursuit of what they thought was worthwhile.

Finally, with *pax Britannica*, various social and religious reform movements and, above all, the national movement for independence, the élites got a much needed reminder to involve themselves in the economic and political issues of society as a whole. The national movement, in particular, led to a clearer appreciation of the ideals of political freedom, electorally mandated authority, responsible and accountable government, and an administrative machinery that was geared to solving the problems of the people. The idiom through which those demands were expressed was that of mass political agitation and non-violent political resistance under the leadership of Mahatma Gandhi. After each round of such resistance, the agitators not only reduced the political distance between themselves and those who governed them but also emerged as individuals, with an increasingly enhanced political capacity.

At the other extreme, in building her participatory institutions, particularly at the grassroots level, the Indians drew heavily on their indigenous experience of participation in the *panchayats,* or local councils, which existed in an uninterrupted manner right through India's long and uneven history. Historians have pointed out that these *panchayats* had turned rural communities into small republics which outlasted several dynasties and empires. In the words of an Indian scholar: "Most of the dynasties in ancient India used to flourish for about two centuries. The village communities and councils were, on the other hand, of hoary antiquity and derived their powers from immemorial custom."[65]

Further, Sir Charles Metcalfe, acting Governor-General of India, wrote in 1930: 'The village communities are little republics, having nearly everything they can want within themselves, and almost independent of any foreign relations. They seem to last where nothing else lasts. Dynasty after dynasty tumbles down; revolution succeeds revolution; but village community remains the same.'[66]

In addition to the twin political heritage, of self-governing rural communities and a mass-based national movement, which regenerated a subject people politically, what gave a helpful start to the future of political liberalism in India was the attitude of the three generations of lawyers (Nationalist leaders over 100 years), and the political élites as a whole, towards liberal political ideals, institutions and practices. They became the founding fathers, and protectors, at least during the critical initial years of Indian democracy after independence.

Apart from their deep respect, bordering on veneration, for liberal ideals, they also came to believe that those ideals had a great role to play in a traditional society like the Indian, with her deeply institutionalised norms of social inequality and associated living. They wanted an ally, as it were, in fighting the social inequality which was implicit in her hierarchical social organisation. And it was their fervent hope that the ideals and practices of equality before law, one man one vote, and so on, would help individuals, especially in the lower social strata, to circumvent the disadvantages of the hierarchy-apportioned privileges and statuses.

But more ambitious, and even radical, was their decision to build a polity of free India round the *individual* in a society which was notorious for its associated living, and which had not experienced the process of individuation which the countries of Western Europe and North America had. In those countries, the individualising experiences could be traced as far back as the Roman Law, certain aspects of feudalism, Protestantism, theories of natural rights, the French Revolution, and, above all, entrepreneurial capitalism from the eighteenth century to the present.

In his introduction to the Balwantray Mehta Committee Report, designed to introduce three additional levels of participatory institutions – at the district, subdistrict, and village levels, which, coupled with the already existing state and union level participatory institutions created five concentric circles of democratic participation – Jawaharlal

Nehru spoke of the waking up of the individual, through various participatory opportunities, and letting him then rebuild his own community.[67]

Even when the constitution of India was being drafted, the founding fathers of the Indian republic, in particular Dr Ambedkar, came out with a strong plea for the rights of the individual rather than an emphasis on associated living.

By any standard, then, the democratic development experience of India has been unique. As compared to the liberal democratic experience of the Western societies, where the growth of capitalism and democracy has gone hand in hand, and the latter is even considered to be a product of the former, the creation of the democratic institutions of free India is the product of the moral and political commitment of her political élites and the drift of her nationalist movement preceding independence. The creation of such institutions of free India was very much a product of the top élites, and not a result of the demands of urban and working classes, as was the case in nineteenth-century Britain.

The Indian situation thus created institutional provisions for effective political participation *in advance* of either a demand for it or the evolution of a commensurate political capacity to influence, and seek response and accountability from, those in public office.

The political capacity of the Indians had either not evolved or was stunted as a result of a series of historical and social factors such as frequent conquests resulting in social destabilisation, a tradition of repressive political authority, and the deeply institutionalised social inequality in her social organisation. This hierarchical social organisation created a peculiar problem. It created what may be said to be a differentiated political capacity to make use of participatory opportunities. Those of the upper castes, often with sizeable portions of land, came in contact more frequently than others with revenue bureaucracy and public officials in general. Such contacts gradually increased their own capacity to transact their business with them. Through such contacts, and through their own relatives in urban centres, those with more education and in the professions, the upper segments of rural India, often got an advance inkling of how public policy was going to change and how they could either benefit by it or protect their own interests. Such segments were also very useful to the electioneering politicians who needed influential men in various rural communities in order to build a patchwork of electoral support for themselves. In return for their services, the individuals in the upper strata of rural societies wanted a suitable modification in the implementation of public policy or a word to the local administrators to 'help' them.[68]

Thus the initial, and continuing, beneficiaries of India's new political system, with its provisions for participation, were those who were in the higher segments of her social organisation. After them came those segments, in the middle rungs of rural society, which stood in a kind of emulative relationship with the upper segments. Such emulative segments came to know about the new opportunities, but always later and always at second hand. The only thing such segments could do was to keep a careful eye on what the upper segments were up to and stay on their heels in the latter's demands for, or utilisation of, new opportunities. But no matter what they did, they could only pick up what was left over.

The middle segments, nevertheless, had an advantage which the upper segment could not match, and that was the strength of their own numbers. Such a strength was obviously very useful to electioneering politicians. But unlike the top segments they were not always able to translate a political advantage into an economic gain and vice versa. Instead there were delays or divisions or a fumbling political initiative which could be warded off by means of 'promises'.

Then there was the lower one-third segment, which, as we shall see in Chapter 3, was the most disadvantageously placed. While it had formal equality, before the law and in terms of vote, it could not translate the strength of its own numbers into political effectiveness. The lower one-third segment of Indian society is further subdivided on caste lines, and the subdivisions are so insulated from one another on the lines of occupations, that it is often unable to generate the political effectiveness to get what was earmarked for it in public policy to 'help' it. The multi-dimensionality of the poor in India, which includes cultural, social, and political factors, along with the economic, as we shall see in Chapter 3, has kept them away from effectively using the newly established demand – response mechanism of her participatory institutions.[69]

The development process in India clearly indicates the need to view it from a more inclusive perspective whereby social, economic and political factors can be considered in the context of such a process, rather than in artificially cut off portions to suit the specialist demands of our various disciplines.

IV SOME GENERAL OBSERVATIONS

Let us now briefly take into account the implications of the variety of development experiences examined in this chapter, for a more inclusive understanding of the development process and, possibly, for development theory construction.

The prolonged historical process of development which character-ises the economic and political growth of industrialised societies, was spread over three to four centuries. It has deservedly become, therefore, a model to emulate, to the extent to which that is possible, for the non-Western societies, which themselves came through an equally prolonged period of internal disorder, imbalances and intrusions. But in such an emulation, and also in century-skipping, so as to catch up with the more advanced countries of the West, the scholars from those countries have begun to realise that given their social and historical background – despite a lot of emulated economic and political institutions – the nature of their own development process must be different. In that connection we made a brief reference to what those scholars referred to by way of the difference in their development process. We also examined the ideas of Max Weber who emphasised the differences in the social and economic background of various Western societies, leading to a variety of capitalist development experiences.

That being the case, we would be much less justified in building a prototype model of the development process which assumed that the sequences of economic, political, social, and other forces were uniformly present in all those societies borrowing Western prescriptions for their own development.

A converse theory, as developed by Myrdal and Moore, referring to the countries of the West, argued that, only after a point, do the forces of economic development so shape the existing legal and political institutions – getting rid of the oligarchic and the archaic – that they, the reconstituted institutions either become 'permissive' of the development process of the capitalist variety, or adjust themselves to it. In other words, an economic phenomenon has now emerged in some of the countries of the West which can reshape and recreate institutions, and evoke the human response necessary to suit its own requirements. And the people in those countries support it for what it delivers in terms of economic growth, political development and social change, all these in an orderly fashion. What we thus have in such a development process is the pre-eminence of the economic factor and its capability to reshape the political and the cultural.

Round such a pre-eminence of the economic phenomenon has also developed, since the English Utilitarians, in the eighteenth century, a corpus of theoretical knowledge – with its own intellectual symbolism, assumptions, abstract set of reasoning, jargon and so on – and a scholarly community with a widely shared confidence in the adequacy of such knowledge.

So far so good. But the problem arises when such knowledge, with all its intellectual machinery and widely shared confidence, is extended to the understanding of the development process in other parts of the world, where the social and historical experience is materially different, and where the economic phenomenon has not yet emerged as the sole determining factor in the development process. As we saw earlier in this chapter, scholars have identified international factors, historical, social and cultural experiences and others, to underline the essential nature of their development experience.

The development process of Western countries, spread over three to four centuries, also crystallised the primacy of the economic factor. Whether we take the writings of Marx, with their dialectical economic relationship between classes, or those of Moore, with much less antagonism between the landed gentry and the peasantry, we get a glimpse of the primacy of the economic factor propelling far-reaching social change in the countries of the West. And although that thesis was partly modified both by Max Weber and Braudel, who wrote about the simultaneous presence of other factors in the early days of capitalism, both of them, nevertheless, also accepted the fact that once crystallised, the economic factor was the major force in the secular or fundamental change in the countries of the West. For such a drift of the development process, the writings of John Locke, with their emphasis on natural rights, and in particular property rights, the spread of Cartesian rationalism, the Age of Enlightenment, the ideals of the French Revolution – wanting to update the archaic social and political institutions – the American Revolution, underlining the importance of participation, all these together supplied the necessary, legal, political and intellectual support. But to presume the presence of such a background in the non-Western countries is to misread what has actually happened by way of their past experiences.

And that is precisely what happens when the corpus of our theoretical knowledge gets formalised round what happened in Western countries, and then gets extended to non-Western countries without much refinement, reconstruction, hesitation or doubt. It then looks for the parallels of Western historical experiences in non-Western societies, and when it does not find them, it tends to ignore whatever is different and even theoretically challenging.[70] It accepts only those theoretical challenges which are based in the shared development experience of the countries of the West. The rest is all exotica for wonder and amusement.

As we saw in this chapter, Raul Prebisch and others were some of the earliest scholars to protest against the neglect of the peculiar development experiences of the countries of Latin America, in their report on behalf of the United Nations. Later on a similar awareness was created by Gunnar Myrdal through his writings. After them, the scholars in various regions became increasingly bold in identifying the peculiarities of the development experiences of their own regions, which were totally ignored by the theoretical knowledge which had grown round what was essentially a Western experience. The Latin American scholars came out with their scholarship of economic history and theory to persuade the scholarly community of the need for the reformulation of theoretical knowledge. The scholars from Asian countries, coming from culturally very different societies, began coming out, gradually, with perspectives on their own development experiences. Unlike scholars from Latin American countries, who shared a number of social, cultural and historical experiences with the countries of the West, those of Asian countries, barring whatever the colonial imposition or deliberate emulation had brought in, had fewer things in common. The culturally multi-layered societies of Japan, China, and India, and the mind-boggling complexity of their development process, were gradually identified and became a matter of real challenge to development studies, which had hitherto merrily sailed into world-wide acceptance along with the Western state system, science, technology, education, political ideals and public institutions. As the scholars from non-Western countries began to delve deeper into their own development experiences, they began to realise how different such experiences were from those of the Western societies.

But unlike the scholars of Latin America, who are anchored in the common epistemological and intellectual traditions of Western Europe, those in Asian countries, with their own deposits of philosophical and intellectual traditions, value systems, social and political ideals, and so on, have a difficult time formulating their own rival theoretical perspectives. For one thing it will require much more time on their part, as the Asian societies are older and culturally far more complex. In the meanwhile what we have done is to glean from their variety of perspectives, implicit theoretical critiques which increasingly point towards the inadequacy of existing theoretical knowledge in development studies.

In all this one thing is certain. The Latin American scholars with their economic history and theories of political economy, and the Asian scholars with their nuanced social analysis of the complexity of cultural life in their regions (which deeply affects their development process), have together posed certain fundamental challenges for the corpus of theoretical knowledge and its claims to universal validity in development studies.

3 The Development Process: A Grassroots Perspective

Let us now examine certain nuances of the development process which have so far received scant attention as a result of premature attempts at theory construction in development studies. Owing to such attempts, not only has the plurality been ignored, but also the complexity of the unique mix of forces which contribute to particular instances of development. We shall illustrate this by taking into account various types of development initiatives: public, private, co-operative, and human self-rebuilding. To allow a closer look at all these, we shall examine them, as far as possible, from a grassroots perspective. With each of these initiatives, as we shall see in this chapter, several factors – cultural, economic, political, human and others – were involved. And regardless of where a development initiative came from, the process which it triggered off had its own unique mix and proportions of those factors. The awareness of such actualities in the development process ought to compel us to engage in a different kind of cognitive effort, by way of development theory, rather than remain anchored in the theoretical corpus developed by the segmented social sciences. And no matter how unprepared we are for such an undertaking, given the fragmented nature of the social science theoretical knowledge to which we are heir, we need to begin somewhere and must hope for an incremental improvement in the quality of our fresh cognitive effort.

In this chapter, we shall first of all briefly mention the resolve of various scholars to go beyond the simple monocausal explanations of the development process, unaccompanied, alas, by any extended work in that direction. After that we shall illustrate a variety of development initiatives involving a mix of different factors.

The chapter is divided into the following parts: (I) the development enmesh, (II) planned development under public initiative, (III) commercial and industrial development under private initiative, (IV) rural development under co-operative initiative, (V) rural poverty requiring a socially concerned human self-rebuilding initiative, (VI) unequal development opportunities and unequal human responses, and (VII) some general observations. We shall now examine each of these in detail.

I THE DEVELOPMENT ENMESH

As we saw in the two earlier chapters, different societies in different regions, at different times, went through different kinds of development experiences. And that is also true of a wide range of developing countries, regardless of deliberate or planned attempts to accelerate their pace of development. Despite development interventions in the form of policies and incentives – given the differences in social and historical background, quality of leadership, visions and goals, ability of the people to pick up new skills – the nature and pace of development in each country, and its various regions and sements, remain different. And we need theoretical formulations to be able to identify, rather than ignore, the essential plurality of their development experiences.

Furthermore, the development intervention in each society, broadly speaking, does not come through a common source. Each society tries out a variety of initiatives and even continues to have them going side by side. Practically all societies, developed or developing, have their own public and private undertakings. On top of those, some societies have a thriving segment of co-operative undertakings. This may still leave a great need for mobilising the lower strata of society, which requires a socially concerned development effort of a special kind.

But regardless of which of the four development initiatives we examine – public, private, co-operative or socially concerned – the cultural, economic, political, and human factors will be deeply enmeshed in that initiative. And while we may wish to isolate each of these factors for our specialist theoretical treatment, as required by our social science disciplines, such an artificial isolation has much less meaning and value within the development process itself. Consequently, when we switch from social science analysis to development analysis, we need to bear in mind that the former has much less validity and justification, because of the enmeshed character of development phenomena. Students of development studies, coming from a social science background, are constantly reminded of how very inadequate are specialised approaches. While the demands of development studies are interactive and holistic, those of the social sciences are segmented and highly specialised.

Let us now briefly examine some of the major thinkers, particularly in economics, who were reluctant to narrow down the range of factors which they thought were pertinent to the understanding of growth or development. The greatest among those is Adam Smith, the father of the discipline of economics. He had the unusual ability to grasp not only what leads to economic growth but also the general principles which can be derived from the understanding of the intricate movement of factors responsible for it. For that purpose Adam Smith identified agricultural surplus as generating a demand for different kinds of goods and services, which in turn gave rise to manufacturing industries and a network of services needed to meet the related demands. The major contribution of Adam Smith was in bringing to our notice the mix of economic and non-economic factors which, together, facilitated economic growth. He argued that as well as a surplus generated by agriculture, we also need a society and political order which subscribes to the view that the personal liberty of the individual is compatible with economic growth. Within such a society and political order everyone would be allowed to pursue, peacefully, his own ambition and avarice. In order to emphasise that point he even declared economic growth, personal liberty to pursue one's self-interest, and a political order which made such a combination of activities possible, the three components of a unified *natural order* with which we ought not to interfere.[1]

After Adam Smith, Ricardo went back to pure economic factors, such as capital formation and the productive power of labour.[2] Then once again, albeit for a short while, the non-economic factors, along with the economic, staged a come-back in the writings of John Stuart Mill. Mill was suspicious of the 'precision in theories about society' and their economic growth, which the classical economists after Adam Smith had formulated. Not only that, he wanted to draw the attention of the scholarly community towards the psychological factors involved in economic growth. He therefore maintained that in the ultimate analysis, the laws of economics are grounded in human nature and therefore in the laws of psychology. He even ruled out the possibility of purely economic explanations of what he called 'practical questions'. In his words: 'there are perhaps no practical questions . . . which admit of being decided on economical premise alone'.[3]

Earlier, we examined the doctrine of Karl Marx, who viewed economic inequality in broad social, political and moral terms, and saw it also as a basic fact governing relationships between classes. The writings of Max Weber, as we also saw, right to the very end sought to identify and examine the large number of factors, including culture, belief system, and historical antecedents, giving different societies a different disposition to economic action. Similarly, the writings of Schumpeter remind us, as we saw earlier, of the fallacy of finding a purely economic source of the economic phenomenon.

Development economists like Gunnar Myrdal, as we also saw, warned against the applicability of purely economic explanations of development to developing countries. The phenomenon of economic growth in the latter had not delinked itself sufficiently from cultural factors. Similarly, Ragnar Nurske came out with a warning against economic analysis of developing countries on purely economic lines and emphasised the need to take into account the enmesh of several factors, of which the economic is one. In his words: 'Economic development has much to do with human endowments, social attitudes, political conditions, and historical antecedents. Capital is a necessary but not sufficient condition of progress.'[4]

Clearly then, there has been a strong tradition of considering the phenomenon of economic growth in its wider contexts, but it has fallen by the wayside. This is clearly seen in the examination of development in non-Western societies where the evidence of cultural factors accompanying the economic, as we saw in the last chapter, is unmistakably present, and yet is often ignored. The reason is that when you admit of the presence of a complex factor such as culture, theorising about development becomes far more difficult. In their 'search for order', to use the expression given by Robert Heilbroner,[5] in the welter of forces which lie at the root of development, scholars have preferred to concentrate on only those aspects, in isolation from others, which lend themselves to a relatively easy form of theorising.

What therefore started off as a broad social approach towards the explanation of economic growth – especially at the hands of thinkers such as those mentioned above, who repeatedly remind us of the deeply enmeshed character of social reality, and, within it, of development phenomena themselves – became more and more concentrated on fewer and fewer variables, so as to make room for the twin imperatives of 'science', namely, measurement and precision.

As opposed to economics, political science, sociology, and anthropology continually broadened their approaches and criss-crossed other disciplines. Only specific branches within them worried about precision and measurement; the rest could live with the ignominy of not being able to become a 'science'. Such a relatively broader approach made them more receptive to the demands of development studies which, as we have seen, call for a more inclusive approach. Such disciplines were much more sensitive to situations of interrelations, interactions, sequences, continuities and discontinuities of various forces, and so on, which characterise the development process.

In the following pages, we shall examine the nature of four different kinds of initiatives in a situation of development stimulus and response. We shall examine, empirically and analytically, the enmesh of social forces within them. As stated earlier, we shall view the interplay of such forces with reference to what actually happened at the grassroots level. My understanding of such a development process is based on field research done in rural and urban communities of western, eastern and southern India over several years.

II PLANNED DEVELOPMENT UNDER PUBLIC INITIATIVE

The decision of the leaders of free India to have a 'planned' development, and within it a mixed economy, did not meet with much resistance. And although in the initial years the private sector in commerce and industry was fearful of the continual harping on the ideology of 'socialism' – which was inspired by the Nehruvian concept of the state as the major initiator of large economic undertakings as well as the custodian of distributive justice – it soon found out that it could continue to exercise influence towards the protection and advancement of its own interests. The same was true in agriculture. The problem for the private sector in a planned economy was, therefore, not one of survival. It was one of influence and how to go about exerting it. What the planned economy thus eventually did was to keep the landed, commercial and industrial interests more or less intact, and to add on top of those a vast bureaucracy, powerful politicians, and middlemen of all kinds to operate its economy.

Given such a mix, the new political economy of India could be explained neither with the help of models suitable for interpreting state undertakings, nor by those for interpreting private undertakings. For it was a mixture of the two together, with an increasing role for the elected public officials, bureaucrats, and an ever more demanding citizenry.

The planned efforts of the Indians in the post-independence period had to address themselves to the many-sided problems of society. The once manufacturing and exporting economy had become largely an exporter of raw materials. The non-responsible revenue collectors in rural areas, appointed during the alien rule, had done a lot of damage to the growth of agriculture. And commerce and industry in general had received great setbacks.

Socially speaking, the problems were of still greater magnitude. The partition of India had left behind a major problem of building a secular society where different religions, after a savage display of brutality, could coexist. Then there was the regional sentiment to contend with. Such a sentiment, based on language, culture, religion, or economic aspiration, could never be ignored. All these, together, created a mind-boggling set of problems for nation-building.

The traditional social organisation of India – involving the multiplicity of religions, and hierarchically ordered social segments, with a near-total neglect of the lower castes, untouchables and tribals – had created for her development resolve a challenge of inconceivable magnitude, especially when all these socially institutionalised divisions were combined with participatory facilities. The task of welding together Indian society, once alien rule had ended, fell on, of all things, the fledgling Indian democracy. The differences had to be allowed to express themselves, first, and then a common ground for their coexistence had to be worked out within a democratic political system. A generation of anthropologically oriented Indian social scientists, inspired by the writings of the distinguished anthropologist M.N. Srinivas,[6] documented, by means of field research in rural and urban communities, the severest tests through which the Indian democratic process passed when it operated in a situation of inconceivable divisiveness, poverty, and illiteracy. It not only survived but went from strength to strength.

In terms of human development, Western education, which only a small proportion of the population could have, had introduced Indians to the achievements of Western countries in science, technology, medicine, legal and political institutions and so on. It nevertheless also made the Western educated minority a class apart, unable to address themselves, at least in the beginning, to the issues of the poor and the socially backward. With all its limitations, however, Western education eventually became a major resource for the Indians to rebuild their society, economy, and polity. It has since continued to play such a role in all compartments of her life.

The various public initiatives in a planned economy came out with much less impressive results, especially in the field of rural poverty, social inequality, family planning, health, and basic needs. Social inequality, in particular, which was deeply rooted in India's traditional social organisation, has been reinforced by the unequal benefits which have resulted during the decades of planned development.

In a situation of antecedent, and deeply institutionalised, social inequality, there was bound to be differentiated use of participatory opportunity and also differentiated response to development stimuli. As we shall see in separate sections of this chapter, both politically and in terms of opportunities offered by planned development, India's better-off segments did much better, often at the expense of those who needed the development opportunity the most.

So while in terms of institutions, goals, policy provisions, and so on, the thrust of development was intended to be pre-planned and controlled, in terms of social consequences of such efforts, what actually emerged was quite different. Planned efforts in fact widened the social disparity which earlier on had been much narrower and confined to the traditional economic and social relationships. What one thus saw in such a development process were the many-sided manifestations of development results, some of them running counter to the intended goals of such an effort.

But what registered itself far beyond the wildest dreams of domestic observers, and outside experts, was the success of India's fledgling liberal political institutions, at *all* levels of her political society. Despite below 35 per cent literacy, close to one-third of people below the poverty line, a deeply institutionalised social hierarchy, and a compliant rather than questioning attitude to authority, the Indians have managed to retain their basic liberal political institutions, learned to use them to protect and enhance their individual and group interests, succeeded in obtaining an increasing measure of accountability from their rulers, totally legitimised the ballot box as the only source of political authority, brought about far-reaching economic, educational and social developments by skilful use of the democratic machinery, and, above all, increasingly made use of the accommodating spirit of the democratic process to meet, successfully, a lot of challenges which came from India's cultural and regional diversity. In such a fundamental development, touching all areas of her life which had registered only limited change over the centuries,

Indian political society went through the usual cycle of crisis resulting from the infractions of her participatory institutions and democratic resilience.[7]

Through her planned efforts, India has also had a considerable measure of success in building and operating democratic institutions in her districts, subdistricts and villages. Over 400 million voters routinely go to polls, in an orderly fashion, to constitute democratically elected political authority at the village, subdistrict, district, state and union level. And looking at the magnitude, diversity, and the backlog of economic and social problems, this scarcely recognised achievement is by any standard one of the greatest political achievements of the twentieth century.

All these institutions, whether economic, political, educational or social, which came into existence as a result of planned effort to serve specific goals, have triggered off processes of development which are many-sided and deeply enmeshed in one another. No matter where you look, one compartment of development process leads to another. In such a process there are also simultaneities, interconnections, interactions, mutually strengthening or weakening effects, with problems of time-lag and/or of halting sequences, in short a process which defies segmented analysis even if it is required by the imperatives of certain social science disciplines.

From the standpoint of the central theme of this chapter, namely the development process, both from the point of view of stimulus and response, and also the need to grasp their interrelations, we find that the many-sided public initiatives had equally many-sided responses which were intricately woven into one another.

Such planned development, in a society which had deeply institutionalised social inequality, seems to have had contrary results in her economic and political field. In the economic field, especially, while India was able to establish her own industrial base, belatedly put emphasis on agriculture and make herself self-sufficient in that sector as well, despite her enormously growing population, nevertheless, the manner in which the planned policies were actually implemented resulted in the reinforcing of the pre-existing inequality. A new class of plan beneficiaries, consisting of industrial and business houses, large landowners, bureaucrats, politicians, power brokers and so on, emerged and benefited immensely from planned public initiatives. In terms of class mobility, more than 10 per cent of the population began enjoying the fruits of affluence brought about by such initiatives. At the other extreme, contrary to the intent of the planned initiatives, those below the poverty line also doubled after those initiatives were introduced.

The widened inequality was of an economic and political nature rather than traditional. Nevertheless, directly or indirectly, it also strengthened the antecedent traditional inequality by adding constraints of a non-traditional nature, over and above the traditional.

Politically, the results of the introduction of participatory institutions within a society with deeply institutionalised social inequality, were of halting sequences and resumptions. With the rural communities, the use of participatory opportunities by the middle and the lower middle agriculturist castes, which were numerically the largest groups, was most effective. They came into public office in villages, districts, and state legislative assemblies. But such a drive fell short of forcing the pace of change in the field of social status. In spite of their enhanced political power, such agriculturist castes were not able to improve, appreciably, their social status from what it was before. They remained where they were in the traditional social hierarchy. There was no doubt widespread praise for those among them who occupied public office. But they needed more than formal power. The sequence of change in their case thus became halting. It might still result in added pay-offs, both in economic and social terms, in the near future.

Some of the social and educational developments also had uneven results from the series of public initiatives. While education and literacy grew phenomenally, building a solid base for a new, and different, kind of society, there was also a continuing loss of highly qualified men and women to industrialised countries, as they could not all be absorbed within India. But the worst losers were the rural communities, and within them the backward social groups. Their educated young men and women continually migrated to towns for office jobs, leaving those communities without much-needed leadership by the educated. Thus in either case, the investment in human development, as launched by public initiatives, benefited the individuals much more than the communities of which they were a part.

One could go on listing instances of broader social consequences of development initiatives, launched by public bodies, which needed careful examination in all their interrelations. While social science disciplines prepare us to look for a specific aspect of the development process, what is needed, in addition to that, is an inclusive picture of the consequences of various development initiatives. Such an interrelated picture of the social consequences of development efforts is more easily identifiable when we consider other forms of development initiatives. To that we now turn.

III COMMERCIAL AND INDUSTRIAL DEVELOPMENT UNDER PRIVATE INITIATIVE

Let us now briefly examine the mix of development factors, and the responses to them, in certain instances of private initiative. In order to examine them intensively, we shall confine our analysis to a small town called Anand, in the state of Gujarat in western India, where I happened to do longitudinal field research. Anand is a flourishing commercial, industrial and educational centre in the region, and, more recently, has become the centre of dairy co-operatives in India.

A century ago, in 1891, Anand, with its population of 9000, came to have the status of an urban municipality. In 1980s, its population, largely due to an influx of people from outside, crossed the 100 000 mark. The ever-expanding rural–urban economy of Anand provided opportunities for private initiatives to its local inhabitants, to those who came from outside, and, recently, to East Africa returnees. Such opportunities were in the field of agriculture, commerce, industry, banking, education and in various professions. For our purpose here we shall analyse the mix of forces which went into private initiatives directed towards agriculture, commerce and industry.

The early years of Anand's economy, barring certain commercial ventures and workshops run by blacksmiths and carpenters, depended heavily on agriculture. The bulk of crops which its inhabitants took from the land were for their own subsistence. The agricultural scene, however, began to change in early 1930s when about one hundred Anand farmers, all of them belonging to the Patidar caste, produced surplus wheat and rice, and sold them in the local grain market. Such farmers became relatively affluent and were dubbed 'progressive farmers' by the locals. In course of time, as the Patidar farmers recalled, their own wants grew and they were, therefore, compelled to find ways and means of getting more out of their land. The reasons for this are discussed below, but the most obvious was social: the Patidars with daughters to marry were under constant pressure to save money for their dowries, a widespread practice which struck deeper roots at the turn of the century. The socially ambitious among the Patidars wanted to marry their daughters to boys from traditionally prestigious villages, and for that they had to provide a much larger dowry. This practice of hypergamy, of wanting to have matrimonial relations above their class and status, forced the Patidars to experiment with different crops and look for a higher rate of return from them. The *social* requirements of such families thus made them develop a different kind of outlook on agriculture. They now not only consulted their fellow farmers, but started seeking help from various visiting officials of the agriculture department, so as to get more out of their agricultural efforts. That led to the establishment of an agricultural research institute in the town which then guided the farmers in matters of seeds, new techniques of irrigation and farming, fertilisers, pesticides, cash crops, switching of crops, getting three instead of two crops per year, and so on. Simultaneously, the farmers' relentless clamour for more water also resulted in the construction of irrigation canals in the region.

Since the variety of agricultural inputs improved the yield on land, more and more Patidars wanted to expand their landholding. In post-independence India, not only were such efforts discouraged, but even existing landholdings came under a close scrutiny with the passage of the Land Tenancy Act. A feeble, and what proved to be abortive, attempt was made under the Act to give land to the tiller/tenant. Because of the political and administrative pressure from the landowners, the Act had very little success.

While the expansion of landholding was not a route which the Patidars could opt for, they could nevertheless go in search of better returns from cash crops. In addition to an earlier switch to tobacco, the Patidars also started growing sugar cane, bananas, cotton, and, more recently, edible oil seeds such as groundnut, sunflower, castor, mustard and vegetables. That led to an enormous production of grains and vegetables in the area, making the town of Anand one of the inordinately large grain and vegetable centres in the region.

With the added growth and greenery on the land, the Patidars could afford to have more milch animals on their farms. But after a few years of involvement in dairying they switched to other ventures, as we shall see later on, in order to get better returns on their investment.

One of the greatest single attractions to the Patidars of staying in agriculture, despite more attractive economic opportunities which the burgeoning town of Anand provided, was the absence of tax on agricultural income. And it is here that the extended nature of the Indian family proved to be a great boon. The enterprising Patidar could ask his brother or cousin in the village to cultivate his land, with the help of agricultural labour, and then move into Anand with his own family so as to undertake commercial or industrial ventures. What such extended families thus did was to diversify their own human resources to different forms of economic enterprise. So great was the benefit of such a diversification that every 'successful' farmer in the region was expected to back up the progression of one or more members of his family towards commerce or industry. While in undertaking such ventures a Patidar no doubt took some risk, nevertheless he also had his land to fall back upon just in case the commercial or industrial venture did not succeed. The closely knit extended family, together with the facility for absentee agriculture, provided the Patidars with a sense of security for new ventures.

After the First World War, members of successful Patidar farmer families went to East Africa, Southeast Asia and other parts of the world, under the compulsion to diversify family resources. But during the last three decades, as the emigration of the educated Indians to North America and Europe grew, the Patidars and their educated children in urban centres also took the full advantage of it and further diversified their family resources. Even abroad, in some cases, the educated Patidars kept up the dynamism of their parents and moved from profession to business or industry, wherever better profits took them.

What is interesting to note here is that in the Patidars' economic drive there were more than economic factors involved. There were the factors of social pressure, of individual resourcefulness, of extended family which served as a cushion against any failure in new enterprise, and, above all, continuing individual drive in ever-expanding national and international areas.

Such a drive cannot be explained with the help of simple arguments relating to a work ethic emphasised by a particular belief system. For the belief system of the Patidars is also shared by a large number of people who are making little progress economically. Moreover, the same Patidars, with the same belief system, were not going anywhere themselves a century ago. What we need, therefore, is the identification of the mix of factors which were responsible for their private initiatives.

In the commercial development of Anand, a number of factors played their part, over and above those identified so far. To a new entrepreneur in Anand, the rapid development of a transport system proved to be a great blessing. It phenomenally expanded Anand's local grain and vegetable market, so that it became the produce market of the region. The development of the road transport system itself was an outgrowth of the co-operative dairying in the district. The prestigious Amul dairy, which came into existence in 1946, covered practically all one thousand villages in the district by mid 1970s. Twice a day, Amul's subcontracted trucks would go to all the villages with empty milk cans and bring back milk for processing in its plant at Anand. But along with empty milk cans, the trucks also carried groceries, cloth, medical supplies, electrical items, bicycle parts, housing equipment and other goods, which the villagers required from Anand. The villages, in return, also sent to Anand their grains and produce.

The railways linked Anand to distant markets in India. Together with the milk and milk products of Amul dairy, the railways carried grains, vegetables, tobacco, fresh lime, fruits and so on, and brought back textiles, shoes, televisions, video recorders, scooters, refrigerators, medical supplies and whatever else the affluent shoppers of Anand needed.

The phenomenal expansion of Anand, especially from the 1960s onward, brought to the urban community additional financial and educational institutions, created jobs in various offices, and attracted a large number of professionals. In wave after wave, there was an influx of teachers, doctors, lawyers, chartered accountants, architects, engineers, mechanics and others. Anand's expansion thus kept up with the enterprising spirit of the Patidars and others.

Let us now briefly look at the changing industrial scene of Anand and its vicinity. Before independence the industrial units of the urban community, and its surroundings, consisted of small casting factories and engineering units. Such units were mostly owned by individuals from the Panchal caste, who are the traditional smiths/casters of iron implements. Despite their limited education and hereditary apprenticeship training, they could manufacture water pumps for which there was a good demand in the surrounding villages. It is said that the Panchals of Anand had installed forty such pumps in the neighbouring villages, and each of them worked without any complaints being made.

The first engineering workshop in Anand was established in 1914, and was appropriately named the Panchal Workshop. It is still a thriving concern. After water pumps, the workshop began manufacturing *bidi* (indigenous cigarettes) machinery, and parts for tractors, trailer«s, and ploughs. The Panchals of Anand were also given contracts to supply parts for the prestigious and ultra-modern Amul dairy.

Until around 1950, one could start a small industrial unit for as little as Rs200 000 and a medium scale unit for Rs500 000. The 1960s saw in Anand the establishment of leading industrial units such as Elecon, Rolcon, Vallabh Glass Works, Comet Paints and Rahul Paints. The liquid cash needed came from agriculture, dairying and commercial income and, above all, from the savings of the Africa returnees.

The Government of Gujarat also wanted to encourage the trend towards the industrialisation of Anand and therefore set up its own Industrial Corporation. The Corporation, in turn, acquired 256 acres of land on the outskirts of Anand and established what came to be known as the Vitthal Udhyog Nagar, named after the illustrious nationalist lawyer brother of Sardar Patel. The industrial site provided facilities for water, power and transport, and in less than two decades the Corporation was able to turn the area into a thriving industrial zone.

The industrialists of Anand are proud of the fact that most of the small and medium-scale industries in the zone are *quality* industries. So great is the awareness of quality and standardisation in that area that many fore««ign firms, including «German and Japanese, operating in other parts of India, subcontract parts which they need to firms in Anand.

The awareness of quality came as a result of the importing of quality material for personal use by people in this region. Whenever a Patidar family returned from the UK or US, it brought with it high-quality equipment for personal or even factory use. That equipment then became a standard to follow when an industrial unit was established.

So far our discussion on private initiative has largely centred round one caste, the Patidars. Another social group which might have been expected to show similar private initiative was that of the Banias or the merchant caste. The Banias did not have a land base, however. They were either in money-lending or in commerce, and the Patidar economic explosion overshadowed their performance in commerce. The bulk of the Banias started as small shopkeepers and stayed there.

In terms of our concern in this chapter, namely the complexity of the development process and the enmeshing of different factors in it, we find that the economic success of the Patidars, and the pressures on them to succeed, had their reasons in what happened to them as agriculturists at the turn of the century. Neither the local historians, nor the professional genealogists, who keep detailed accounts of people's movements, speak about anything extraordinary happening to them at that time. And still there was a surge of many-sided activity, including economic, on their part.

One of the explanations of pressures on them to succeed economically can be found in the formation of matrimonial groups, locally known as the *ekadas*. The story begins further back, however. At the turn of the century, six of the Patidar villages, namely Sojitra, Karamsad, Nadiad, Bhadran, Vaso and Dharmaj, happened to put relatively greater emphasis on education, and produced educated men, who were then employed in government service. This was then regarded as an important position to have, and subsequently more young men from those villages received a good education and found higher positions in government and the professions.

Coupled with that was the traditional prestige of those villages. Sojitra is a very old village and is supposed to have figured in Ptolemy's astronomy as 'Sojitrus'. A few Nadiad Patidars are supposed to have sailed to England in a country craft to meet Queen Victoria, to plead for the restoration of their rights and privileges as traditional village headmen. Similarly, others of the six villages also had distinguishing stories to give them high status.

The next thing we know is that they started claiming that their honour was higher than that of other Patidar villages. They thus became what is locally known as the *mota gams* (prestigious villages). After a few years of such claims, the six villages constituted themselves into an *ekadas* (matrimonial circle) of their own. They also announced that they would marry their daughters only within those villages. However, girls from other villages could be married to boys in the *mota gam*, provided an adequate dowry was given. This triggered off a panic formation of other *ekada* which were known by the number of the villages which first constituted them, such as *moti satyavis, nani satyavis* (big 27, small 27) and so on. Each of those subsequent *ekadas* in fact had more Patidar villages than their names suggested.

From then on, the average Patidar family was forced to earn more and save so that its daughters could find a suitable match in marriage. At just about the same time we see a great improvement in Patidar agricultural performance and also the undertaking of risk, notably going to East Africa and Southeast Asia to make money.

The growth of such an entrepreneurial character, in what was traditionally an agriculturist caste, thus had some social dimensions to it, which concerned matrimony and social status, over and above the economic. That explained the early part of Patidar's economic drive. And later on in their development, the economic factor itself became powerful enough to sustain such a drive.

Since the economic performance, or the lack thereof, of other castes in the region was tied up with dairying and subsistence farming, we shall take up their pattern of economic initiative in the next section.

IV RURAL DEVELOPMENT UNDER CO-OPERATIVE INITIATIVE

Let us now briefly examine the nature of the development process set into motion by co-operative initiatives in the field of dairying, and lately in edible oil seeds, in India, and the different social, economic, organisational and political factors which they brought into play. The milk co-operatives, in particular, are considered to be the greatest success story in rural development since independence. In four decades, they have made India the third largest dairy country in the world. By 1989, her milk output had reached 46 million tons a year and was thought likely to double in the following ten years. It is also expected that milk will become, in the near future, the second largest agricultural product in India, second only to rice.[8]

Although the milk co-operatives are primarily economic organisations, in their establishment, operation, and participation a number of other factors have played an important part. In the following pages, we shall examine the mix of several factors in the development process initiated by India's four premier milk co-operatives, namely Amul, Dudhsagar, Sabar, and Sumul, all of them in Gujarat in western India.

Let us then begin with Amul. In a literal sense it was an offshoot of the Indian national movement. Its groundwork was laid by the topflight leaders of the movement, such as Sardar Patel and Morarji Desai. Subsequently, district level leaders mobilised the farmers, while socially concerned dairymen, technologists, veterinarians, procurement officials, and technocrats gave an organisational shape to some of the vague conceptions and ideals of co-operative dairying which had emerged in the early days. In addition there were the grassroots leaders and farmers who were willing to try out a new organisational principle and learn from its many-sided implications for a wider notion of rural development.[9] Thus in both the establishment of co-operatives and response to them, a large number of factors were involved.

The fact that the milk co-operative movement began with Amul, located in Kaira district, can be understood with reference to the surplus of milk in the region. The prosperous agriculture of Kaira had enabled its farmers to maintain a large herd of milch animals, most of them buffaloes. They used to convert the surplus milk into *ghee*, purified butter, and ship it to the nearby city of Mehemdabad which had become a flourishing centre of *ghee* trade at the turn of the century. Buyers used to visit it from as far as Calcutta, Delhi and Madras.

Then agents of small dairies in various urban centres, including Bombay, came to the district to ensure the supply of milk. Some of them were also the suppliers of milk and milk products to the British army. The more trusted among these was Polson dairy, which was encouraged to expand its business by having a processing plant in the city of Anand itself. Thus came into existence the well-known Polson Model Dairy, which was supposed to be the most modern dairy in the whole of Asia.

With the outbreak of the Second World War, the milk contractors and, in particular, Polson, obtained from the government of Bombay the exclusive right to milk collection in the district, at a price determined by themselves. Polson, together with various milk collecting contractors, made huge profits at the expense of producers. The producers were unhappy with the constraints imposed on them and therefore repeatedly took their grievance to nationalist leaders such as Sardar Patel and Morarji Desai. Because of their deep involvement in the freedom movement, those leaders could not immediately pay much attention to the farmers of Kaira district. But in 1946, a year before India got her independence, they organised a strike by the farmers of the district. Fourteen villages participated, and their leaders were arrested. Very little milk could reach Polson, and the army barracks.[10] Finally, the government of Bombay agreed to the farmers' demand that they supply milk to their own co-operative organisation, which could then sell to whichever client it wanted. Thus came into existence, in 1946, Anand Milk Union Limited, in short AMUL. It was destined to become one of the greatest farmer owned and operated milk co-operatives of the world.

Although several attempts had been made from the 1930s onwards, for co-operative marketing of agricultural products, especially in the Surat district, this was the first time that farmer producers, rural leaders, and dairy technologists had come together to build the new type of co-operative organisation. Later on they were joined by more professional people in the fields of both production and marketing.

While the producers as individuals wanted to eliminate the middle-men, they could not do it unless some leaders at the district level organised them for such a purpose. And those leaders by themselves could not build the organisation unless they could get the dairy technologists, veterinarians, extension and procurement officials, and all those who had specialised in the new technique of packaging and marketing to join them. For a society which had been through a period of prolonged subjection, and was also notorious for its extreme form of individualism, the convergence of efforts by farmers, rural leaders, and dairy technologists, within a co-operative framework, was indeed a remarkable achievement. For what they set out to achieve with a co-operative initiative was far more complex and difficult, in terms of development process, than what was undertaken by either the public or the private initiative. In a co-operative initiative it is necessary to build a mutually beneficial relationship between the various groups of actors involved or else they will start functioning at cross purposes.

A highly respected district level leader, Tribhuvandas Patel, who came through the mill of the Indian national movement, and V. Kurien, an engineer turned dairyman with a genius for building highly practical organisations, together, in a rare partnership spread over three decades, launched the co-operative initiative of Amul, which soon became a household name in the vast stretches of India.

Amul was able to attract a group of highly dedicated veterinarians, dairy technologists, engineers, and extension workers. And through their concerted efforts, over three decades, it was able to establish milk co-operative societies in practically all the villages of the district. By means of its veterinary services, animal health care and artificial insemination programme, it was able to increase not only the milk yield of the animals but also change the quality of livestock in the district.

When Amul began, most of its membership was drawn from the ranks of medium and large landowners. In course of time they moved to cash crops in agriculture and their place was taken by small and marginal farmers and landless labourers. By the mid 1980s three-fourths of the membership was drawn from the small, marginal and landless farmers. And by 1988–9, Amul was able to inject into the economy of the district more than US $100 million a year, by means of the sale of milk and milk products to urban centres in India. By any standard that was a remarkable achievement.

While the makers of the earlier village milk co-operatives were the district level leaders, their work was subsequently taken over by the veterinarians. They went to different villages and talked to their residents about how their milch animal would improve in quality if they became recipients of Amul's veterinary services by joining the Co-op. But the greatest contribution of those veterinarians was in targeting the poor, the very poor, and the resourceless, for joining the milk-producing community and thereby supplementing their limited income. To conclude this point, one of the most important features of the co-operative initiative was the human intervention by socially concerned dairy personnel. Without their intervention, co-operative dairying would have simply remained a preserve of the better-off farmers. More about that later in this chapter.

But what made the structure of Amul unique was its emphasis on the participatory mechanism at the village, district or union level, and, later on, at the level of the milk marketing federation. Its founding fathers believed that unless farmers were given a sense of participation, they would not be interested in scrutinising the performance of their organisation, nor would they be able to seek the accountability of their executive personnel. The co-operative network established by Amul, and later on by similar co-operatives in the neighbouring districts, helped strengthen, the democratic process at the grassroots level, as we shall see in detail.

Amul caught the imagination of Prime Minister Lal Bahadur Shastri, who briefly came to office after Jawaharlal Nehru. He wanted Amul, or what came to be known as the 'Anand Pattern' to be replicated in 400 odd districts of India. He therefore helped establish the National Dairy Development Board (NDDB) in Anand, and Kurien was appointed its chairman.

Fortunately for Kurien, in late 1960s and early 1970s, European countries had an unsold stock of butter and milk powder. He therefore persuaded them to donate as well as sell a part of it. When that was done, Kurien made an ambitious plan, called *The Operation Flood*, to build milk co-operative organisations in other states of India, on the Anand Pattern. With funds generated by the sale of butter and milk powder, he was able to give initial financial and organisational help to various states. The western and the southern states of India, after an initial resistance, adopted the plan and made a great success of co-operative dairying. Among the rest, bureaucrats, administrators and politicians, who did not want to share power with grassroots organisations, continued to obstruct its penetration. However, from 2000 co-ops in 1970, the NDDB was able to build 55 000 milk co-operatives by 1988, benefitting 52.5 million small farmers of India.[11]

One of the earliest beneficiaries of the Operation Flood was Dudh-sagar Dairy, in the town and district called Mehsana. Dudhsagar's quantitative and qualitative performance in many respects excelled that of Amul. This is because after nearly four decades of continuous growth, there was an inevitable decline in the *élan* of Amul.

Dudhsagar benefited from the trial-and-error procedure of Amul so far as the organisation of the network of village co-operatives was concerned. It then went beyond that. Besides productivity, it concentrated on targeting women and the lower castes for development. Attention to both these groups meant that its personnel, right down the line, got deeply and personally involved.

Unlike the Kaira district, where Amul holds jurisdiction, the district of Mehsana has poor quality soil and very little water. To compensate, it had its own valuable resource, namely the Chaudhuries, an agriculturist caste, and in particular their women, who became legendary breeders of milch animals. The breed of milch animal used is locally known as the *mehsani*, and the Chaudhury women had brought that animal to perfection.

Mehsana also produced its own highly effective team of district level leaders, who then worked with an equally dedicated team of technocrats, veterinarians, and procurement officials. Together they were able to stimulate, catalyse, and build village level leadership in community after community in rural Mehsana. Even in the 1980s, one could see in those rural communities a level of social idealism comparable to that among the top flight leaders of the Indian national movement before independence. And their excitement in building and operating a new economic organisation in the district, which was farmer-owned and operated, had no parallel in the post-independence India.

In a span of a few years, the Chaudhury women, with the help of a highly active and research-minded veterinary personnel, were able to enhance the productive capacity of the *mehsani*. Within a short period, it was a common sight to see the animal giving 12 to 15 litres of milk after its second lactation, with fat content ranging from 6 to 9 per cent. The Chaudhury women also took great interest in experiments in artificial insemination on their animals. The idea was to improve not only the milk productivity of the animal but also to shorten the period after which the first conception would become possible. For that purpose the Chaudhury women became, in their cowsheds, a kind of an operative arm of the veterinary research scientists.

Then came the big switch from the *mehsani* buffalo, an animal which they had known for generations, to the high yielding cross-bred cows. The cross-bred cows which gave 20 to 25 litres of milk per day, started improving in their performance and the best among them reached 45 litres per day. No one could argue against that level of success, and the Chaudhury women, after an initial resistance, started saying goodbye to the familiar *mehsani*.[12]

In two decades after its establishment, Dudhsagar started registering an explosion in its milk productivity. In the second half of the 1980s, Dudhsagar started earning for the district close to US $100 million from the sale of milk and milk products. What is more, some of its milk-producing rural communities became what may be appropriately called *the mega milk economies*.

The earliest to come up with such a stunning performance was a village called Pamol. In 1988–9, Pamol, with a population of 6000 crossed the magical figure of Rs 1.17 crore, or US $0.70 million per year. That was a huge amount for a rural community. Close to one-third of the population of the village consists of Chaudhuries, and it was in this village that the Chaudhury women had started working actively with veterinary personnel, setting an example for women in other rural communities to follow. It was also in this village that the leaders saw to it that a co-operative fodder farm was developed on the village *gauchar* (village common), so as to enable the landless also to have milch animals: in return for working on the farm, they got wages, and also fodder at a reasonable rate. Within the district Pamol thus became a symbol of what the villagers themselves could do for their fellow poor.

Bapupura is another rural community, with a population of 2200 (1988). It is almost entirely inhabited by Chaudhuries belonging to two lineage groups. In 1988–9, it came out with a stunning production of milk to the tune of Rs 7.4 million or approximately US $0.50 million. The extraordinary thing about Bapupura is that nearly three-fourths of its co-op membership is drawn from marginal and landless farmers. The village does not have many people with leadership quality, but has instead a traditional social cohesion which has helped it to operate its co-operative organisation in the most efficient manner.

There are now nearly ten rural communities which, like Pamol, are nearing milk productivity figures of Rs 1 crore or US $0.75 million. All of them have a sizeable population of Chaudhuries, the great animal breeders. One rural community which does not have such a composition is Boratwada. The proportion of Chaudhuries there is much less, but its Chaudhury leadership has used the principle of co-operation to help the community fight against the natural disadvantage of extremely poor soil. It has surrounded the community with concentric circles of co-operatives ranging from milk, edible oil seeds, agricultural implements, consumer goods, and, above all, water. In a community of 2000, it has been able to have six co-operatively owned bore-wells and twenty group-owned wells. Boratwada has thus put to extensive use the very principle on which co-operatives are based. It would be difficult to find another rural community in this region which tried to overcome the setback of low natural and human resources (it has a far bigger component than other villages of backward social groups) by latching itself on to the co-operative principle and making it work, economically, to its own advantage. The leadership of Boratwada played an equally important part by welding the disparate fragments of an economically and socially backward community into a well-oiled co-operative machine.[13]

The liquidity generated by Dudhsagar for the district of Mehsana began to have a cumulative effect on its agricultural economy. The availability of liquid cash, earned through the sale of milk, all the year round, helped farmers to switch their transactions from credit to cash. It also helped them to experiment with cash crops and vegetables as they were able to install more bore wells, use more electricity to draw water, and employ more labourers than before. In 1989, it was estimated that the district had nearly ten thousand bore wells, which made it one of the foremost bore well districts in India.

The availability of additional water also meant more greenery and more farm cuttings. A part of such cuttings was claimed by landless labourers as a component of their wages. Locally it was known as *bharo*, the headload. The *bharo* helped the landless labourers to maintain a milch animal and thereby supplement their income.

At the other extreme of the agricultural economy there were certain families which were able to diversify their economic resources by starting commercial ventures in nearby small towns such as Vijapur, Patan, Harij, Kheralu and Kadi. As in the case of Kaira Patidars, few Mehsana Patidars or Chaudhuries set up commercial ventures for the enterprising members of their family without giving up their land, which was then looked after by a close relative. The bulk of the new shopkeepers in those towns were essentially those who had come up the dairy-agriculture ladder.

Then there was the flourishing milch animal trade in the district. Earlier certain villages had specialised in sending milch animals to the *tabelawalas*, or cowshed owners, in Bombay. By law such a trade required permission but certain individuals in those communities had found a way round it. While the milk-producing peasantry in the district frowned upon such practices they could do precious little to stop them. Later on some more villages sprung up as centres of cross-bred cow trade in the district.

Since women were the mainstay of the dairy industry, Dudhsagar started targeting them for a more comprehensive role. They were enrolled along with their husbands as members of the milk co-op. Between them, husband and wife had only one vote. It was presumed that they would vote together. Women were also made the joint beneficiaries of insurance on the animals, and joint owners of animals bought through loans. Women rather than men thus became the targets of all the extension workers in the district.

Such an involvement of women, together with the linkage between women and the vets that we noticed earlier, began changing the women's outlook. In less than a decade after such changes were introduced, more women were seen in public meetings and in decision-making bodies.

The impact of Dudhsagar on the agricultural economy of the district of Mehsana was different from Amul's impact on the district of Kaira. Under the impact of Amul a kind of *social queue* had emerged in the dairy economy of the district. Some of the upper castes which had entered the queue first, seizing the early opportunities in the development process launched by co-operative dairying, later moved out into enterprises such as cash crops in agriculture, and also commercial and industrial ventures in nearby towns. The vacuum left by their exit was filled by caste groups which were traditionally lower than their's. The upper castes did not move out totally or suddenly from their top position in the queue, however: only the proportion of their investment in milch animals declined. Since they could get much better returns on cash crops and commercial ventures than on dairying, they made use of family manpower and fodder on the farms to maintain an optimum number of animals. Thus the district of Kaira, with its economically mobile caste group, and the liquidity afforded by dairying, built, first of all, an agricultural then a commercial and, finally, an industrial component into its economy.

The agriculture-cum-commerce-cum-industry profile of Kaira district, under the impact of dairying, was at variance with Dudhsagar's impact on its surrounding rural communities. The district of Mehsana, as stated earlier, did not have good soil nor enough water to be able to build its own agricultural base. Barely two decades ago, one could see barren stretches of land almost all over Mehsana. That landscape has changed substantially. The bore-wells, bought largely with the help of liquidity from milk, have created a large number of pockets of greenery, and experiments in various cash crops, including edible oilseeds, have increased farmers' income. A number of rural communities have come to the conclusion that they cannot get more out of land because of its inherent poor quality, so their investments have continued to be in milch animals. Returns from cross-bred cows, particularly, have been more than helpful in sustaining their interest in dairying.

Moreover, the district of Mehsana has a large number of Chaudhuries, who (especially their women) are deeply devoted to dairying. It is not certain how long that will last, however. The Chaudhuries are a close variant of the Patidars as an agriculturist caste and, as such, stand in an emulative relationship with them. It remains to be seen whether the Chaudhuries will start imitating the Patidar movement from dairying and agriculture to commerce in a big way. If they do, the character of the district's economy will change substantially.

As of now, under the enormous impact of dairying, the district of Mehsana has gotten into a dairying-agriculture-dairying cycle. The bore-wells bought with the help of milk liquidity create more greenery and fodder, and this additional farm cuttings help maintain more milch animals. That in turn further increases the income from milk, helping still more bore-wells to be installed, leading to a greater availability of fodder and then to the possibility of having more milch animals. Such a cycle has been most beneficial to the district and its growing population. The oil and natural gas strikes in the district, although a big public undertaking, however, cannot sustain the increase in its population.

With the Sabar dairy, in a district adjoining Mehsana, called Sabarkantha, we come to yet another development profile. The youngest of the premier dairies of western India, Sabar came into existence in 1968. In the winter of 1985, it drew the attention of the Indian dairy community by saying 'no' to the purchasing and processing of nearly one-fourth of the milk that the rural communities in the district produced. This was because the milk production in the district had far exceeded its processing capacity. Estimates of capacity and its gradual expansion were based on an outdated study. The problem in this was more than the phenomenon of milk glut which occurs in winter months, and which is known in dairy lingo as 'flush season'. For Sabar a glut was threatening to become a continuing problem.

Sabar's development as a milk co-operative had had to wait for a prior development of agriculture in the district, and the critical point at which it could begin sustaining an increased number of milch animals. The co-operative is located in a small town called Himmatnagar which, before independence, was the capital of a princely state. The district of Sabarkantha was carved out of many such small princely states, whose princes and their feudal underlings, known locally as the *darbars*, did not bother to develop agriculture in their territory. On the eve of Indian independence the princely order became nervous and started selling land in panic for as little as Rs 50 per acre. The people who bought such lands were prosperous Patidar farmers from Kaira, Baroda and certain areas of Kutch.

Such farmers sent managers to hire labourers and cultivate crops. In a few cases the owners also migrated to Sabar, but neither the owners nor their managers wanted to live in the villages. They therefore settled on their own large pieces of land, and around their houses sprung up the huts of their agricultural labourers. Such settlements were known locally as *lats*, and their owners, as *latwalas*.

The district is dotted with *lats*. Nobody knows their exact number but various estimates put them at somewhere around two to five hundred. They are in a sense the new villages of the district, some of which are still not on the revenue list. The new agricultural development has taken place round these *lats* and they have given a great stimulus to the agricultural economy of the older villages of the district.

The commercially minded, sometimes brutal agricultural managers of the *lats* were not always popular with the old villages, but since they gave steady employment to the landless population of such villages, the criticism of their highhandedness was often muted. The *latwallas* levelled the land, brought in topsoil, bored for water, experimented with crops, and in the shortest possible time, created green fields out of barren tracts.

Initially, they did not favour dairying as they needed buttermilk, along with the midday meal, as a part of the wages to be given to their labourers. But when their capacity for sustaining more milch animals increased, they became ardent supporters of the dairy industry in the district. The other dairy-supporting component was the resident Chaudhury population of the district. The Chaudhuries of Sabarkantha, in terms of both their interdistrict social status, and their skill in breeding animals, were several cuts below the Chaudhuries of Mehsana. The Mehsana Chaudhuries accorded respect to only a few Chaudhuries of Sabarkantha, which resulted in the formation of the restricted matrimonial relationship between them.

The Chaudhuries of Sabarkantha were however reputed for their willingness to have apprentices in their cowsheds. Consequently, a large number of lower caste and tribal boys picked up skill in animal-keeping from their Chaudhury gurus. In fact the contrast between tribal villages with a Chaudhury component, and those without, makes a very interesting study. The tribal villages with a Chaudhury population, and therefore scope for apprenticeship in animal keeping, came up very rapidly in dairying. Those without it did not.[14]

One of the subdistricts of Sabarkantha, called Prantij, has a large population of Patidars. They already had a co-operative dairy structure before Sabar came into existence. Consequently, Sabar was able to build on the available co-operative structure and the experience of the locals in operating it. While the Patidars of Prantij were moving more towards agriculture and vegetables, they had not totally divested themselves of dairying. Their political leadership at the district level was also most useful, until other backward social and economic groups in the district started competing against them for political power.

The most numerous group in the district was that of the Kshatriyas, but they were far too used to looking to the *darbars*, the feudal lords, for economic and political lead. Over the years the *darbars* had become defunct both economically and politically, but the Kshatriyas were slow to realise, unlike their counterparts in other districts, that they themselves could fill the vacuum by means of a greater involvement in the public affairs of their rural communities. They have increasingly become aware of such a responsibility but have yet to act on it.

The development character of the co-operative initiative undertaken in the heavily *Adivasi* or tribal populated district called Surat, where Sumul dairy is located, is different again. Nearly 60 per cent of the population of the district consists of the *Adivasis*. And while some of the non-tribal sub-districts – consisting of Patidars and Anavil Brahmins, with recently provided irrigation facilities and resultant cash crops such as sugar cane and bananas – have registered economic prosperity, those in the Adivasi sub-districts have continued to live in abject poverty. Over thousands of years the Adivasis dodged their incorporation into the broader Indian society and retained their cultural identity by living in inaccessible hilly tracts or forests. They therefore remained outside the mainstream of Indian social and economic development.

Sumul dairy, after establishing milk co-operatives in the non-tribal subdistricts, wanted to penetrate into the tribal belt. Its reason for doing so, at the organisational level, was to get more milk to satisfy the ever-increasing demand from the burgeoning city of Surat where Sumul is located. Surat, the second largest city of the state of Gujarat, has gone through different waves of prosperity. After being the art silk capital of India, it became a home of small scale textile industries, putting out of action the large textile mills of Ahmedabad. That phase was followed by the establishment of a diamond polishing industry which is said to earn close to a billion dollars, officially, for the district, and unofficially perhaps twice as much. The villages of Surat district are now dotted with electrically run wheels for cutting and polishing diamonds. All these waves of prosperity resulted in a demand for more milk and the city of Surat was prepared to pay about the highest price in India per litre of pasteurised milk.

When Sumul was established, the people who needed the least development stimulus from it, initially benefited the most. The antecedent social inequality within the society had ensured a differentiated ability to benefit from the development stimulus provided by Sumul in the early years of its organisation.

Sumul was heir to a rich historical tradition of experimenting with co-operatives. The ideal of a co-operative alternative for the Indian economy was ever present in the thinking of the nationalist leaders when they were fighting for independence. As early as 1928, they had launched the famous Bardoli *satyagraha*, a non-payment of taxes protest, against the alien rule, in one of the villages of Surat district. While the co-operative movement never got off the ground, there were a number of short-lived attempts at constituting co-operatives for fruits and vegetables. But all such experiments were conducted by the rich farmers for their own benefit.

When Sumul dairy was established, the rich farmers were all too eager to join it. Initially, Sumul had to amalgamate the existing co-operative structures already established by them. Such farmers resisted the idea of giving loans for milch animals to the landless labourers (the tribals). The rich farmers were worried that they might lose a source of cheap labour for their farms. Sumul could not therefore reach the landless labourers who worked on the farms of prosperous Patidar and Anavil landowners, but it was, nevertheless, free to move into a large number of tribal villages, in the bulk of the sub-districts.

There too there were some problems. Traditionally the tribals had no experience of dairying. Those who had cultivated a taste for milk, did not as a rule have the capacity to own an animal. Moreover, the men and women had no familiarity with the work associated with the maintaining and milking of the animals. The task of penetrating the tribal villages fell on the veterinarians. They did the extension work in those villages, hiring Rabari (the traditional grazers and keepers of animals) women to teach tribal women how to milk animals. During such exercises tribal women often complained of aching fingers which were unused to milking. Then the tribals had to be taught how to measure fat content and above all, how to keep books.

Under the new rural development policy, money was provided towards loans for milch animals when the tribals needed them. Since most tribals lived on the edge of forests and on hilly tracts, they could usually find some fodderland for their animals. Besides, some of them owned small pieces of land which could also sustain animals. Finally, the cohesiveness of tribal villages, and a relatively narrower gender distance in their social organisation, proved to be of immense value in establishing milk co-operatives. The milk co-operatives of the tribal villages worked with much less friction, than those elsewhere and the women in them, without encouragement by extension work, participated in deliberations and held elective positions. More than a quarter of the membership of tribal co-operatives consisted of women.

By 1985, Sumul, with the help of its socially concerned veterinarians, was able to establish milk co-operatives in nearly 600 tribal villages out of a total of 651. By that time three-fourths of the total milk collection of Sumul dairy was coming from the tribal villages. In a span of fifteen years the tribal villages, through their self-involvement, had undergone a double revolution. First of all they had become milk producers, which they never had been before. And, second, they had become the mainstay of the milk-producing community which a modern dairy organisation in an urban centre needed.

The tribal social structure, and its cohesiveness, had almost assured the successful operation of a co-operative organisation. Those villages did not have the problems and tensions which caste villages had. Moreover, their relatively narrower gender distance, whereby women worked side by side with men in almost everything, created a much more realistic atmosphere in the co-operatives. Then there was the relatively strong ethic of repayment of loans among the tribals, which ensured the near-total recovery of loans given to their villages, and that too in the shortest possible time.[15]

In helping the tribals build their milk co-operatives, a variety of socially concerned individuals and organisations were involved, over and above a massive undertaking by the veterinarians of Sumul. Each of these human initiatives left behind its own imprint on the tribal community. We shall examine certain aspects of such imprints in the next subsection. First though, another co-operative venture should be mentioned.

Until a few years ago, India was self-sufficient in edible oil. But then, due to the increase in her population and the rise in her standard of living, she began to import either edible oil or oil seeds. The question arose as to how to persuade Indian farmers to increase their productivity. Apart from various agricultural inputs, including soil testing, research in improved seeds, and the use of fertilisers and pesticides, there was the problem of marketing and getting an adequate return on the crop. Oil seed production, processing and marketing had so far been in the private sector. Due to manipulation of market prices by the 'oil kings', and the connivance of politicians, the farmers did not have much incentive to increase their production. It was then asked whether a co-operative organisation could take up not only the purchasing, processing and marketing of oil seeds, but also the organisation of various inputs at the village level; and it was decided that the National Dairy Development Board, which had done highly impressive work in milk, should be asked to take over such an assignment. The Co-operative League of the United States of America (CLUSA) and the Canadian Co-operative Association (CCA) agreed to give the necessary aid to develop such co-operative organisation at the grassroots level.

After their initial teething troubles, largely due to bureaucratic delays in putting the necessary organisational structure in place, and vested interests which were threatened, the oil seeds co-operatives took longer than expected to get off the ground. Their performance varied in different parts of India. They usually did much better in areas where there was previous rural co-operative experience. In others the participatory and accountable character of these grassroots rural oil seeds co-operatives had an electrifying effect on the outlook of the farmers. They now wanted other co-operatives to be organised on similar participatory lines. Apart from the better returns to the farmers for their crops, these participatory organisations, as in milk co-operatives, have strengthened the democratic fabric of rural India. Farmers, big and small, are induced to get involved in the participatory process, and thereby learn to protect their own interests. However, since the entire co-operative initiative in the field of oilseeds is of recent origin, its impact on the development process of rural India has yet to be studied intensively.

V RURAL POVERTY AND HUMAN SELF-REBUILDING INITIATIVE

Let us now briefly examine some instances of efforts of socially concerned individuals who have sought to involve disadvantaged individuals in their own development rather than make them the mere recipients of the provisions of public policy. Such a human initiative was primarily concerned with the building up of the social and political capacity of those segments of society which, for a variety of historical and social reasons, were unable, on their own, to get out of the state of economic backwardness, social indignity, and political incapacity. In order to illustrate this, we shall take the examples of a variety of efforts made by a range of socially concerned individuals in rural Gujarat, to help the poor and the very poor to break out of their social and economic constraints. As mentioned earlier, each of such efforts left behind its imprint on the people whose development it sought.[16]

We have already noted that there is much more to the poor than their economic deprivation. The phenomenon of poverty, when looked at closely, turns out to be a many-sided problem. In different societies

one can find, along with the economic, different reasons why their poor
remain poor. But within the poor of those societies there is always a
core which benefits less than any other group from the provisions of
social policy, even when these are directed specifically at them. Such
a core needs the intermediary of human agency to prepare it to claim
those provisions and, in course of time, become the 'demanders and
takers' of what has been officially provided. For such a shift the poor
have a lot of 'growing up' to do from a condition or a situation which
– because of a many-sided assault on their person and dignity – has
stunted them. They therefore need a many-sided development, and
not just economic relief: the all-round development of the poor just
does not take place if they become the mere recipients of the public
largesse distributed through bureaucrats. That growth can only be
achieved by involving the poor and the disadvantaged in their own
development, and thereby helping them catch up, as it were, with the
rest of society. The only assured route to their development is their own
self-involvement, but to get to that critical point, they need, initially
the helping hand of socially concerned individuals.

This point is vividly brought home to us when we take the example of
the poor and the very poor in rural India. Their incapacity to get out of
their condition of backwardness is indeed many-sided, and those many
sides reinforce one another and make the escape of the poor from their
condition of poverty and indignity that much more difficult.

Since the dawn of Indian civilisation the poor have also been the
lower castes, the untouchables, and the tribals. While students of
the social sciences have singled out the economic factor from the
rest, those trying to understand the complexity and actuality of the
development process cannot realistically do so. And since the better
off, along with the poor, are given to explaining poverty with reference
to one's *karma*, or past births, very few of them feel morally obliged to
treat it as a social problem or a matter of shame. On the contrary there
is always the deadly conviction in rural India which can be summed up
as 'there always will be poor'.

The poor, on their part, have also internalised their own insignifi
cance and marginality to the rest of society. Very few of them believe
that all the planned efforts, targeting the poor for development, are
for *them*. In village after village in different parts of India one
unmistakably hears the view that such efforts are only for the better
off in the community. Such a sense of marginality, implying that they
do not matter to the wider community, has also prevented them
from developing their own social and political capacity, by involving

themselves in the participatory process, and then going after what has been provided in public policy for them.

Now let us examine the results of some of the efforts of socially concerned individuals to involve the poor in their own development. The four milk co-operatives of western India, that we discussed in the previous section, witnessed efforts made by a variety of socially concerned individuals to involve the poor in their respective districts in the participatory and/or economic opportunities provided by the co-operatives.

The two socially concerned organisations, one run by Jesuit missionaries from Spain, and the other run by Manav Kalyan Trust, worked in the district of Surat to involve the tribals in various development opportunities, including milk co-operative dairying. Both of them unfortunately practised different forms of development paternalism with the result that those whom they served remained their dependent wards. The poor did not develop or change from their condition of backwardness, but remained unable to make it on their own after an initial helping hand by these two well-meaning organisations.

In the same district (Surat), at the other extreme there were the Gandhians, including the militant Gandhians who were also the followers of Jayaprakash Narayan (JP). The Gandhians and, more particularly, the JPians, involved the tribals themselves in various participatory and development opportunities, and gradually turned them into self-respecting but politically demanding individuals. Their economic progress coupled with growing political articulation, was seen as a threat by the local Congress bosses in the district. Consequently, by means of administrative machinery, those bosses tried to put various kinds of obstacles in the way of the tribals' development, but with only limited success.

Finally, in the Dudhsagar, Sumul, Sabar and Amul milk co-operatives, and in that order, there were a number of top executives, veterinarians, technologists, procurement officials, extension workers who, for reasons of their own, started adopting specific villages, and within them targeting the poor, for further development. Wherever such individuals were involved, the poor of those rural communities came to participate fully in all the decision-making occasions and development opportunities in general. Such people were constantly required to move to different rural communities, but they, nevertheless, kept an eye on the work that they had already started. In such communities the backward segments, after an initial helping hand from the socially concerned dairy personnel, got the opportunity to stand on their own feet. Their self-involvement had thus become a means of continuing self-development. It was in such communities, due to human initiative by socially concerned individuals, wanting to rebuild the self-esteem and social and political capacity of the disadvantaged groups, by involving them in their own development process, that one could see a marked difference in the all-round development of the disadvantaged.

The need for a self-rejuvenating initiative, implying self-involvement on the part of the economically deprived and socially disparaged individuals, is of special significance to most developing countries and in particular to India. For various historical and social reasons, the social inequality in India is deeply institutionalised. And while the various religious, social, and political movements of the nineteenth and twentieth century, followed by participatory mechanisms provided by the various institutions of democratic India, reached roughly the top two-thirds of Indian society, the one-third at the base of the social and economic hierarchy remained tied to the constraints and incapacities to which the traditional society had condemned it. This segment had to grow into its own full humanhood and be recognised by the other segments as having done so. That could not have been done by making the members of that segment the mere recipients of what the public policy had to offer. Apart from their own economic and educational development, they had also to emerge as individuals in a wider social, psychological and political sense.

Mahatma Gandhi had understood the peculiar requirement of the lowest segments of Indian society, and he therefore wanted a massive internal national movement to address itself to it. He could not persuade Nehru to share his perception of such a requirement, however Nehru followed the institutional and policy route, but the Gandhian perception of the problem came back to haunt him in his declining years in office. Nehru's former comrade-in-arms in the struggle for freedom, JP, who later on became his critic, had repeatedly reminded him of the inadequacy of his approach. But Nehru was too firmly set in his views of planned economic development as capable of bringing about the necessary social change in Indian society. The only concession he was willing to make was in the field of grassroots democratic decentralisation. After Nehru, the groping and ailing JP could achieve precious little. But he did plant the seeds of what needed to be done in the minds of a large number of socially concerned individuals who have since been anonymously involved in such activities in different parts of India. Although inadequate, given the enormousness of India's problems, JP's legacy, nevertheless, has kept a light burning, and has sometimes attracted the unlikeliest of people. The socially concerned co-operative dairy personnel are some of them.

VI UNEQUAL DEVELOPMENT OPPORTUNITIES: UNEQUAL HUMAN RESPONSES

Let us now briefly examine the complexity of the development process, especially at the grassroots level, in the various initiatives that we examined. In each of those initiatives we identified the deep enmeshing of cultural, economic, political and human factors. The responses to those initiatives, as we also noted, were many-sided. And even if we were to isolate one of the sides or factors involved, for our specialist social science treatment, the very exclusivity of such a cognitive exercise would introduce an element of distortion into the situation that we sought to understand. It is all too easy to isolate factors for the sake of our cognitive convenience and not for the adequacy or depth of understanding.

The variety of initiatives that we examined in this chapter drive home the point that cognitive exercises which depend on the exclusivity of specific factors, rest on the false assumption that development phenomena can be viewed independently of the antecedents, contexts, and interactive forces of which they are a product. Only for our initial analytical distinctions and exercises – and also to meet the specialist demands of the social sciences which developed before the different kinds of demands of development studies were recognised – can we engage, justifiably, in the exercise of analytical purity. Some of us also continue to remain bound to the segmented and contextless approaches because despite all our dissatisfaction with the existing intellectual approaches to development studies, not much else has appeared, so far, as an alternative.

Viewed from a grassroots perspective, the majority of public and private initiatives, resulted in what Mahatma Gandhi had called a governance from 'a distant centre'. In such initiatives, the rural communities, where the bulk of the population lived, were merely at the receiving end, rather than active participants in making decisions and formulating policies which affected them. In post-independence India, the urban bias (and increasingly more and more of it) in various sectors where development efforts were launched, was all too familiar to the grassroots communities. Such communities had resigned themselves to the fact that their lives and conditions would go on, despite development noises to the contrary, as before.

But it was not as simple as that. A variety of efforts introduced by 'the distant centre', required a variety of adjustments on the part of the grassroots communities. While in response to some of the measures introduced from the top, the rural communities were forced to take cognizance of what was expected of them, in others their social and economic reality gave a peculiar, even local, character to the operational aspect of whatever was sought to be introduced. Let me briefly illustrate this.

The various segments of the rural community were 'rattled' or frustrated when some of the earliest public initiatives were introduced by the state governments in the form of land tenancy laws. The idea of making a tiller the owner of land, whether he was a share cropper or tenant, rattled the landowners. They had to pull a lot of administrative and political strings, indicating dire consequences, especially at election time, if certain escape routes were not provided. Village after village failed to produce the intended result. And land continued to remain in few hands in rural India.

On either side of the land tenure divide, however, the rural communities learnt a few lessons of far-reaching importance. One was that the interventionist government, both at the union and state level, had something either to give or to take away from them. Another lesson was that the battle for it could be won or lost not only in the arena where public policy is made, but also in the way it is implemented. The successive provisions of agricultural credits and inputs, water resources, pricing and the like now became subject of a lot of trade-offs. Despite all the pious professions of helping the poor, in the actual application of public policy the better off, and sometimes the least needy, were the great beneficiary. And so far as the lower social and economic strata of rural communities were concerned, they were not always able to translate their anger into alternative political choices, given their sense of marginality, political incapacity and gullibility.

While the large landowners, given their economic muscle, sought security through their political influence, and the middle level land-owners, given the advantage of their large numbers, sought it through political participation, the lowest one-third, which had neither the economic muscle nor the political capacity, nor indeed unity, merely continued to remain the wards of those in power, as they always had done throughout Indian history. The social consequences of various public initiatives thus further accentuated the disparity in economic standing and political influence which had already existed in unequal traditional society.

Politically speaking, 'the distant centre' had sought to alter, radically, the way in which political authority, at the village, sub-district, and district level, was constituted. The centre now wanted the right to govern to be based on the numerical electoral support enjoyed by individuals contesting for public office, replacing the right to govern that was based on traditional social and familial status. One of the greatest political dramas, involving a shift of political power in post-independence India, was in her age-old local institutions, the *panchayats*. Earlier, they had served as participatory institutions based on the consensus of various segments of rural society, but always under the stewardship of people with higher social and economic background, and senior in age. Under the new system, the panchayats' political power shifted to those who could build a patchwork of political support and thus achieve a wider consensus, based on the accommodation of views and interests of the others.[17]

The shift from the traditional way of constituting political authority to one that involved the electoral mechanism was never explained to rural communities. There was some explanation of it in urban centres, but hardly any in villages where four-fifths of the population then lived. They learned about democracy, or *lokshahi*, by involving themselves in the democratic process itself. In this, however, their own heritage of *panchayat*, together with the ideals and goals of the long-drawn out Indian national movement, proved to be invaluable.

But what no one could tell those rural masses was the dos and the don'ts, both normative and pragmatic, of operating the fragile institutions of democracy. Once again the urban dwellers had some advantage over the rural. The nationalist leaders of post-independence India, lawyers, teachers and others, addressed several meetings in towns. But the rural communities had to learn by themselves, often by going to their traditional moral notions of right and wrong, in order to evolve their own sense of how to operate the newly established liberal political institutions.[18]

At the other extreme, through various planned public as well as other development initiatives, the traditional isolation of Indian rural communities was becoming a thing of the past. The proliferation of administrative machinery, economic and political linkages, and ever-expanding road, rail and communication facilities began to nibble away at such isolation.

As a result of the many-sided development stimulus, what began to emerge was a city-linked and dominated, rural–urban society, with its own intricately interwoven responses. Prior to the launching of public initiatives, there was the traditional social organisation which had registered very little change, an agricultural economy ravaged by colonial administration, and a citizenry with a stunted political capacity. But after many-sided public initiatives, India's political and economic society became a complex of relationships, forces and interwoven social consequences, to which mutually isolated social science subdisciplines and their theoretical separations, with their roots in the historical and social experiences of the Western development process, could do little justice. Clearly then, what was required was another round of cognitive thrust of a different kind.

In the domain of private initiatives, at the grassroots level, again, only those segments of traditional society benefited which could either continue or build on their traditional occupations by taking the advantage of the new opportunities. Such segments, by and large, were confined to the upper strata and their respective occupations in the traditional society. Since, in the lower strata, the bulk of social segments were in the traditional service sector (with a few exceptions), they had hardly any new opportunities come their way. Let me illustrate this.

One of the interesting factors to examine in the Indian development process, is how different caste groups – with traditional occupations and certain kinds of economic activity permitted to them – benefited by the modernisation thrust.

The traditional priestly and scholarly occupation of the Brahmins, involving individual initiative, did not always reward them financially. They gained much more when they bought land and/or entered the money-lending business. But such opportunities, and others like becoming advisors to kings, came only to a few of them. During the period of modernisation, after the arrival of the British, their traditional emphasis on education helped them to increase their educational qualifications and get into various professions or work in offices.

The Banias, the merchant caste, continued and contrived on their traditional occupation of trade, commerce and money-lending. Some of them then graduated to another but related economic form, namely industry. With their private initiative, they became the largest single group of industrialists in the country. In a sense the Banias of India built on their own traditional economic occupation, and benefited the most by the enormous opportunity provided by the accelerated pace of development in India after independence.

However, the most innovative group, which continued and adapted substantially its traditional occupation was that of the Patidars, discussed earlier in this chapter. Given the various development opportunities, the Patidars moved from agriculture to commerce and then to industry without giving up any one of those activities. Theirs is a unique example whereby a people made an economic success of all the major forms of economic activity. No other caste group came close to them, not even the Banias, for they did not have an agricultural base to their operations.

The close variants of Patidars were the Chaudhuries, who found their *métier* in dairying and to a limited extent in agriculture, as we saw in the section on co-operative initiative. So far the Chaudhuries have made use of the development opportunities offered by dairying to make phenomenal progress. This they have done by continuing their traditional economic activity of animal breeding and improving the breed by means of modern veterinary science. But they have not gone beyond that, at least not for the present.

The Chaudhuries, however, stand in an emulative relationship with the Patidars. While they (the Chaudhuries) have found a new economic *niche* for themselves in dairying, sooner or later they would like to go the way the Patidars went. There is evidence, especially in the small towns of Mehsana district, that some Chaudhury families have undertaken small commercial ventures without giving up dairying or agriculture. It will be interesting to observe where they go from there.

The economic dynamism of various social segments in the traditional Indian social structure, in the face of development opportunities, begins to decline (barring isolated cases) once we go below its middle agricultural strata, occupied in the western region by the Chaudhuries. We then come across another agriculturist group called the Kshatriyas which in the past also acted as soldiers. They are, as we saw, highly leader-oriented and look to the *darbars*, the feudal Rajputs, for economic as well as political leadership, in which the latter have done badly. And now it remains to be seen whether the Kshatriyas will begin looking to the Patidars or Chaudhuries, as their economic role models. Politically speaking, the Kshatriyas, who are the largest numerical group in the region, have emerged as a group which, to some extent, is now independent of the *darbars*. But this is yet to be matched by them in the economic field.

Lower than the Kshatriyas, in the traditional social hierarchy, few castes got new economic opportunity during the accelerated pace of development in post-independence India. The Prajapatis, or the potters, could make use of their traditional experience of working at the wheel in recently started diamond-polishing factories in the villages of Surat district. But in this they have to compete with young men from the higher castes. Then there are some Prajapatis who have continued their traditional occupation by going into modern bricklaying and ceramics, but these are very few indeed.

Below them are carpenters, blacksmiths, barbers, washermen, and the whole range of still lower castes, and then various segments of the untouchables, who did not get any development opportunity to put to use their traditional occupational skill. The entire development process seems to have bypassed them.

Among the untouchables, only one group, the Venkars, refused to accept their traditional economic destiny of weaving which suffered enormously as a result of the growth of the textile industry. Instead they put great emphasis on education and started sending their young to urban centres for office jobs. In recent years, some efforts have been made to involve Venkars in the weaving of specifically designed material, such as shawls and baskets, for urban use. But such an involvement is very limited indeed.

Private initiative for development, as could be expected, has had unequal results. During the period of accelerated development process, apart from individual differences, some occupational groups got generally better opportunities than the others. And so far as groups in the lowest strata of traditional social organisation were concerned, no development opportunity came their way which they could have used to improve their condition.

The co-operative initiative, by providing liquid cash, catalysed the economic potential of various social groups. To begin with it provided a kind of a social queue, as stated earlier, whereby the economically stronger and socially higher groups got in at the top of the line, followed by the others in the social hierarchy. The liquidity provided by the dairy industry helped the Patidars to switch to cash crop agriculture and then, in some cases, helped them move on to commerce and small-scale industry. The co-op dairying helped the Chaudhuries to find an economic niche for themselves. Since dairying has phenomenally expanded, with better and assured return on investment, the Chaudhuries benefited immensely from what they were good at. The dairy industry, as a development opportunity, seems poised to get a more effective response from the Kshatriyas. Lower down the traditional social and economic hierarchy, its catalytic potential was more and more limited. The two social groups it was able to help were those of the Venkars, the ex-untouchables, and the tribals, particularly in Surat district. Of the two, the Venkars had longer experience, and greater benefit, of dairying. With the help of the additional cash they earned, some of them bought more and better animals, and, in certain cases, extra pieces of land, but because of their social stigma they did not feel that their children would have an economic future in the village. They therefore planned for their children's migration to the cities, by giving them a better education.

This then brings us to the social consequences of the self-rebuilding initiatives that we examined. The nature of social inequality is complex and many-sided, and it cannot be explained in simple economic terms. As we saw in the section on human self-rebuilding initiatives, the poor and the very poor had many more disadvantages, and constraints, to their possible development than one could identify by means of economic categories. Their all-round state of disadvantage and underdevelopment was in fact a product of a number of reinforcing factors, such as economic resourcelessness, low traditional social status, deep belief in *karmic* rationale, to the point of accepting whatever was offered to them, a deep sense of marginality from the main stream of society, and a political incapacity to fight back, within a democratic system, for their due share of development provisions. What they needed was not something that could be given to them with the help of bureaucratic machinery but an opportunity and a participatory process for self-involvement in getting what was earmarked for them. Only through such a self-involvement could they also bring about their own self-development. Since the dawn of Indian civilisation their process of growth as individuals was truncated because of their exclusion from the main stream of society. It was therefore necessary to build them back, as it were, to their full humanhood.

And that was by no means a simple process of acquiring economic resources, or the vote or an altered cultural identity by means of new surnames. The Venkars of Gujarat, the Mahars of Maharastra, and the Ezvas of Kerala had tried all those things, and still they needed to grow in their own self-esteem by achieving what could not be easily ignored by others, namely an all-round development.

VII SOME GENERAL OBSERVATIONS

Let us now build a few general arguments relating to the enmeshed character of the development process, which seems to get chopped up in order to suit the specialist requirements of our social science disciplines.

Broadly speaking, nearly all developing societies now have valuable experiences of development with their own proportion of successes and failures. They also have experience of development efforts which, in some cases, increased the economic disparity, and social and political distance among the different components of their societies. Such a fund of experience is far more valuable than a newfangled theory, a faddish model, or an obsessive perspective of bright people in various international development agencies. For experiences of development efforts, including failures, will not be a total write off if valuable lessons are learnt and practical insights gained from them.

And as the foregoing pages have indicated there are always many more reasons for growth wherever it has occurred, than the presence of policies and economic stimuli. Conversely, where growth has not occurred uniformly in the same society there are diverse reasons, arising out of social and economic unevenness which prevent a uniform response to development stimuli. Consequently, both for growth and non-growth, we need to look at a far more diverse group of development factors than our social science disciplines prepare us for. Since development as well as non-development calls for wider social explanations than the mono-causal ones we are used to in our social science disciplines, it might be a useful exercise, at least initially, to treat them both as products of a group of factors in an effective/non-effective mix of proportions. After positing such a plurality of development resource – and not the function of any single factor such as savings, work ethic, free enterprise, liberalism or modernity – we can then turn our cognitive efforts to knowing more about the proportions of the development mix, given the specific social situations, which have or have not worked in different kinds of development experiences. In other words, we need to look again and again at the plurality of factors, mix and proportion of factors, specific social situations, and the results that they produce in different development efforts.

The four development initiatives that we examined from the grassroots perspectives in this chapter, indicated a complex intermeshing of economic, social, political and human factors.

The various public initiatives which sought to reshape the complex of economic, political and social relationships at the grassroots level, had made a difference to only a part of them, leaving the communities to generate their own internal dynamism to extend that process to the other parts. Whether it was policy concerning land tenure or elected local councils, or the implementing of the various provisions of social policy, the unique response of each rural community was based on its own social and economic composition and leadership. While in broad terms the rural communities, appear to have responded uniformly to the institutional and policy stimuli introduced by various public initiatives, in actual practice there was a uniqueness in the response of each determined by its own internal composition.

Much greater variety was identifiable, as could be expected, when we examined the responses of certain segments of the community under private initiative. Within each of those responses, once again, the inevitable mix of cultural, economic, political and human factors was unmistakably present.

In that particular context we also considered the concept of *continue and contrive*, indicating that private initiative favoured, as it were, people in those occupations which were fairly high up, thereby suggesting a link between an individual's position in the social hierarchy and the various development opportunities that routinely came in his or her way. No doubt there was also the factor of individual initiative in grabbing such development opportunities, but most of those opportunities did not go much below the traditional occupations of the middle castes.

The co-operative initiative helped by catalysing the economic drive of some, finding an occupational *metier* for others, and creating new opportunity for still more. There too the individual's traditional occupation furnished him/her with the ability to innovate, find an appropriate vocation, or just miss development opportunities that come in his/her way.

Finally, the human self-rebuilding initiative, with an initial helping hand from socially concerned individuals, also indicated that the mere presence of development opportunities, so far as the disadvantaged segments were concerned, was not enough. Initially they needed a human agency to help them utilise those opportunities.

All these then point to the fact that the human factor, as shaped by position in the traditional social hierarchy and the specific occupation that it prepared an individual for, also oriented an individual's response to development opportunity. What we need, therefore, is a nuanced analysis of the specific social situation of each segment of society, if we are to understand their differing response to development stimuli.

But within all these elements what is most difficult to identify – after we have established the pluralist argument of the presence of a diversity of factors both in development stimuli and in development response – is the nature of interrelations, interactions, emulations, continuities and discontinuities, sequences, leaps, limping dynamics, and dead ends, all these, as components that our renewed theoretical effort ought to pay attention to.

All that we can do at this stage of development studies is to resensitise fellow scholars to the broader contexts which surround the development process, and to the need to grasp interrelations between the processes of development and the contexts within which they occur. And then wait till our understanding of the complexity, plurality, and interrelationality of various factors in the development process reaches a critical point from where our renewed effort at another and, more informed, round of conceptualisation can begin. For too long we have followed an exclusively speculative route to the understanding of the development process. The time has now come to balance it with a deeper understanding of the development experience that is now available, before we prepare for the next round of our cognitive effort at development theory construction.

4 Dimensions of Development Theory

Let us now examine the theoretical significance of the diversity of development experience of different societies, their socially and culturally shaped processes of economic and political development, and then identify within such processes the core issues which lie at the heart of those societies' development in general.

In any attempt at development theory construction – which after an initial speculative effort, gives way to an inductive probing into the actualities of development processes and experiences, and thereby constantly engages in refining theoretical formulations themselves – we face a number of problems. As a consequence of Western dominance, we have got used to the notion that all societies, sooner or later, will evolve economic and political institutions similar to those of the industrialised countries of the West. Such a view gets reinforced at the hands of the corpus of theoretical knowledge in the social sciences, which tends to see the parallels, attained or evolving, of the Western economic and political institutions and practices in developing societies, and often ignores most of the actualities and specific directions of their development processes. So very deeply ingrained are such assumptions, in our existing theoretical knowledge, that neither our academic critiques nor even our field research findings and reports, have been able to build adequate defences against them. And despite our dissatisfaction with the state of development studies, and the periodic self-criticism of our own approaches, we almost always seem to go back to doing what we did before.

Moreover, the manner in which our social science knowledge has developed, largely by chopping and slicing the social reality, so as to suit the specialist requirements of each of the branches within the social sciences, is not very helpful in development studies, which, after a span of similar fragmentations, is now crying out for a more inclusive and integrated perspective on some of its own unique problems. But what is worse, in order to perpetuate their approaches, even when they are extended to development studies, justifiably or otherwise, the proponents of the main body of theoretical knowledge in the social sciences tend to look down upon anything 'interdisciplinary' as not rigorous enough, and therefore devoid of intellectual respectability. Such notions of academic respectability have often discouraged scholars from looking into the complexity of development processes – with their mind-boggling plurality, interrelationships, interactions, sequences, continuities, discontinuities and so on – from a more inclusive perspective. The standards and directions set by the disciplinary specialisations of the social sciences have thus been strictly adhered to even in the applied field of development studies. In fact development studies, so far, has not been allowed to emerge as a discipline with unique problems of its own. In such a social science invasion of development studies, while the former has gained some newly colonised territory, the latter has lost the very scope for evolving its own unique, and intellectually adequate, approaches to the different kinds of problems that it has to deal with.

The other problem that arises in any attempt at development theory construction lies at the very heart of the kind of *theory culture* that has been created within the social sciences. More often than not we like to guess our way into social reality by means of speculative attempts, rather than weave a picture of it by means of a series of initial speculative theories, further refine those theories in the face of challenges, and then under the direction of the refined theories identify empirically grasped fragments of social reality, and, finally, piece them together by means of expanding concentric circles of general arguments. In terms of theoretical respectability we are conditioned to regarding theory-directed empirical knowledge, excepting at the hands of great masters like Aristotle, Marx and Weber, as strictly second rate.

Such a theory culture poses a serious problem for development theory construction. For development theory, or for that matter development studies, are largely about the non-Western societies, the cultural complexities of which we are gradually beginning to grasp through disciplines such as history, anthropology, language, religion and so on. The most valuable resource for our theory construction, as we saw earlier, is development experience itself. We need to pull out fragments of that and put them in the ever-widening parameters of our understanding of them before we build theoretical arguments to capture, as it were, their interrelated character and essence.

The development experiences of those societies also stimulate our thinking on what I have called certain core issues which we ought to address our cognitive efforts to. Such core issues, which have many universalistic and particularistic attributes, need to be identified.

Together, these then become the several dimensions or aspects to which any attempt at development theory ought to address itself. In the following pages we shall examine some of them. The chapter is divided into the following subsections: (I) plurality and diversity, (II) development complex and continuum, (III) development core, (IV) ethnodevelopment, (V) back to the conceptual drawing board, and (VI) an inclusive and incremental exploration of development theory. We shall now examine each of these subsections in some detail.

I PLURALITY AND DIVERSITY

As the arguments and critiques in the foregoing chapters suggest, the emphasis on the segmentation of theoretical knowledge, together with the assumed universality of the development experience of various countries of the industrialised West, was misplaced. What was required instead was a differentiated and nuanced social analysis of the actual development experiences of different societies, with the help of a refined or reformulated body of theoretical ideas which was capable of handling the unfamiliar and interrelated aspects of their development processes. The segmented theoretical approach may have suited industrially developed societies, especially in view of the fact that such societies were able to 'delink' their economic growth and political development from their wider cultural contexts; nevertheless, it is woefully inadequate in explaining the development processes of those societies where cultural, economic, political and human factors are intricately interwoven. Whenever such segmented theoretical approaches tried to 'fit' any artificially chopped-up aspect of the development process of developing societies into their own specialist requirement, the results had the look of a development unreality. It often sounded clever, to have undertaken a cognitive exercise of an abstract variety to explain an unfamiliar and exotic society, but it was not very meaningful to the world of actual development experience.

The segmented theories of development, embedded in various branches of the social sciences, and their perspectives on development process, failed to produce the inclusive approaches which the development studies required. Specialist after specialist neatly sliced off, from an already artificially chopped-off portion of development phenomena, whatever his or her independently developed intellectual machinery could manage. Thus only those intellectual formulations which could be derived from a reigning theoretical model or a temporary fad in the social sciences were considered to be intellectually worthwhile or respectable. In contrast, there were fewer instances of scholars going in search of what their specific themes in development studies demanded, unencumbered by the theoretical popularity of certain approaches. Often, research approaches were shaped or even dictated by what was popular in the mainstream social sciences at any particular time and, therefore, facilitated research funding.

Thus the perspectives on development studies, and specialists' interest in them, were often limited in advance of research, not by the complexity of development phenomena themselves but by the various theories and models in vogue in social science disciplines, with their intellectual respectability, opportunities for travel and working in different places, and, above all, acceptance and security among a community of scholars. By oneself, in the hazardous terrain of research, one could perish. To anchor oneself in the mainstream discipline was therefore the safest thing to do, quite apart from the intellectual respectability it gave.

Periodically, when the disciplinary approaches were castigated for having engineered a tunnel vision of development studies, one could join the chorus of collective disapproval. Simultaneously, one could also join the chorus of appreciation of the views of Weber, Schumpeter, Myrdal, Hoselitz, Hirschman and so on, suggesting that there was something limiting in the way social sciences have gone about their business in development studies – and then go back to one's research approaches as before.

Repeatedly scholars from different branches of the social sciences, interested in parallel or similar aspects of development processes, met with the theoretical shields and armour provided by their respective disciplines, and either politely ignored each other or ridiculed the 'unsoundness' of each other's approaches, and then parted company. They often heard nothing and learnt nothing from one another. Theirs was, at best, a dialogue of the deaf and, at worst, an intellectual exercise in mutual recrimination and futility. At the end of each such encounter most social scientists vowed to have nothing to do with the other side of the disciplinary divide.

What we now have by way of development studies, as pursued by various branches of the social sciences, therefore, are the fragments of the phenomena of development which different discipline-embedded approaches have *carved* out for themselves. In carving out such territories those approaches have their own jurisdictional problems of common themes and issues, problems of overlap, and border skirmishes, but as long as a healthy mutual indifference or tolerance prevails, situations do not become ugly. Moreover, since each discipline-embedded approach is fortified by its own corpus of theoretical knowledge, there is always a feeling of intellectual self-sufficiency, with an assurance that there is nothing to learn from the other side. Rarely do any practitioners of the disciplines, even when they are doing development studies, look at what other disciplinary approaches have to offer. And even when one does pick up some ideas from the other side, they are immediately translated into one's own disciplinary lingo. Thus the field of development studies, instead of becoming a distinct area in its own right, because of its peculiar problems, gets incorporated, in portions and slices, into various branches of the social sciences, with economics getting away with the biggest haul.

The discipline-bounded approaches within development studies have prevented us from looking into the residual, and hitherto untouched, areas within them. Despite nearly four decades of scholarly effort by some of the best minds in the social sciences, we could neither come out of the mire of disciplinary fragmentation nor could we get down to questioning the adequacy of some of the conceptual frameworks which are exclusively rooted in the social and historical experiences of Western societies.

Moreover, most of the disciplinary theories, pressed into the service of understanding non-Western societies, manifested yet another limitation. Since such theories were given to a reductionist bias, they also brought to bear such a bias in development studies, thereby often going in search of simplistic monocausal explanations of complex development realities. With such a bias there was room neither for plurality, even of close variants, nor for diversity, which, by definition, is plurality of unparalleled or distant variants.

The reductionist demands of discipline-oriented development theories imposed the virtues of monistic narrowness on the continuing theoretical explanations, almost always ignoring the complexity of the phenomena in question. Instead of emphasising the time-honoured virtues of simple theoretical expressions of complex situations, a trade-off was entered into which did away with the actual diversity and plurality of the complex and many-sided development problems of the emerging world, in return for the simplicity, and supposed effectiveness, of reductionist theoretical arguments.

What all this has obscured is the fresh demand placed on our cognitive efforts by the very nature of the problems faced by emerging countries. Simply put, the problem we now have is of recognising the essential differences between societies, and of considering how their historical and social experiences shape their developmental problems and, in turn, make fresh demands on our conceptual and theoretical exercises and approaches.

Barring a few exceptions, the simplistic and reductionist exercises in theory construction for development studies were extensions of social science theories themselves. Because of their source, they came to acquire instant intellectual respectability, regardless of their effectiveness or sensitivity to actual problems of developing societies. And then, as in the social sciences, the making and remaking of development theories became an academic ritual. Theories came and went not because of their ability to illuminate the complexity or the actuality of the development process in any particular society but because, as in the case of cars and clothing, styles and fashions had changed.

If such theoretical exercises had confined themselves to seminar rooms, as necessary tools of learning, then the justification would have been more than adequate. But precisely those makers of untested theories, and their students, were called upon to formulate policies, based on such theories, for developing countries which either needed expert advice or had such advice forced on them by aid-giving agencies.

As we also saw in Chapter 2, despite various theoretical contributions made by Western, Latin American and Asian scholars, emphasising the fundamental diversity of development experiences, calling for a commensurate theoretical effort to explain them, the mainstream social science theories, as applied to development studies, remained either indifferent to such contributions or paid little attention to them.

Even the writings of such major scholars as Max Weber, Braudel, Schumpeter, Schweinitz, Myrdal, Tawney, Hoselitz, Moore and Hirschman did not do much to sensitise social scientists to the social and cultural diversity influencing the development process of different societies differently, and which, in turn, required different kinds of theoretical efforts to understand them. Instead the mainstream social science theories, and their universalistic assumptions, prevailed.

Broadly speaking, there have been distinct and identifiable development experiences in the industrialised Western world, in the countries of Latin America, and in the countries of Asia. And scholars working in various branches of human knowledge have collected impressive historical, cultural, social, economic and political data on them. Before long we shall see similar works on the countries of the Middle East and Africa. As our empirical and historical scholarship of developing countries (including the efforts of indigenous scholars), advances, we continue to identify still different kinds of complexity in the development processes of those societies. These become indispensable sources for making any theoretical argument about the distinctness of development processes. Such a realisation ought to have raised questions about the assumption of social science theories that economic growth and political development, everywhere, have been able to 'delink' themselves from social and cultural factors just because that is what may have happened in the countries of the West. Finally, this should have countered the claims to universal validity of theories of development which were almost entirely rooted in the development experience of a few industrialised societies of the West.

In the last four decades, since the publication of the UNCLA report in 1944, Raul Prebisch and other scholars have sought to correct the impression, in the field of political economy and political history, that you can study the development of Latin American countries independently of the actual international economic relationships which have been there since they were colonised. Any attempt to 'delink' their development process from their own historical experiences, just in order to extend the validity of the mainstream social science theories to that region, does not make much sense.

Similarly, in the countries of Asia, such as Japan, China and India, with their own development process deeply enmeshed in their cultural life, as we saw in Chapters 2 and 3, the existing development theories, based on the apriori assumption of the fact of 'delink', make still less sense. The thick layer of culture, which permeates those and other societies in the region, calls for a different kind of theoretical effort from any we have been able to offer so far.

All these then point to one thing: that we need to go beyond the initial Western theoretical explorations and tentative efforts to seek the validity of such explorations to other regions. Our understanding of the plurality and diversity of development processes in countries outside the West has unmistakably pointed out the untenability of such extensions. Moreover, as increasing regional scholarship sensitises us to the basic differences in development experiences, from region to region and society to society, the more urgent it becomes for us to get down to the task of rethinking and reformulating our initial theoretical efforts to face the challenges of the newness of such experiences.

As we also saw in Chapter 2, the variety of development experiences, despite being ignored by reductionist theories, firmly registered itself in the writings of social and economic historians. In a sense, historians, who were not forced to build general theories at the end of their works, but rather to come up with conceptual relationships backed by historical evidence, were more at home with the diversity and plurality of development experiences. But the bulk of their fellow scholars in the social sciences, given the demands of reductionism in their intellectual tradition of theory construction, remained far more concerned with the formulation of general theories, of presumed universal validity, even if it meant the ignoring of facts of plurality and diversity in the experiences of different societies.

Within the social sciences proper, nevertheless, there was also a group of scholars who took up the challenge of historical and social plurality in the development process of various countries and wove into their theory construction various cautionary qualifications. Such qualifications, they maintained, were necessary before one entered into theory construction about the development of different societies. Prominent among them, as we saw earlier, were thinkers like Max Weber, Gunnar Myrdal, Bert Hoselitz and Albert Hirschman. For them those theoretical arguments of the social sciences which ignored the basic fact of differences between societies and their historical experiences were based on distorted foundations.

The pluralist challenges which the historians and a few social scientists of the nineteenth and twentieth century faced, are now being reconsidered by anthropologists and field research political scientists who have come face to face with the diversity of social and development experiences of different societies. As field researchers, neither group could ignore what confronted them in their scholarly pursuits. Both groups also refrained from engaging in sweeping generalisations about societies without taking into account their essential differences.

Once again the debate about the need to pay attention to the plurality and diversity of various societies has erupted, this time around development studies. And if the development studies succeed in staking a claim that they should be recognised as a specific field, requiring a different kind of cognitive effort, rather than be devoured by the social sciences and their theories, which were formulated largely to interpret the social and historical experiences of a few Western societies, then such a debate will not fade away. Moreover, the challenge posed by scholars from the developing countries, bringing to bear deeper understanding of the uniqueness of their own development experiences, despite many an attempt to ignore or stifle them, will not let this debate go, this time around, before development theorists have paid attention to the fact of the essential diversity of development experiences.

II   DEVELOPMENT COMPLEX AND CONTINUUM

As we saw in Chapter 3, a development effort, regardless of the source of its initiative, has in it a mix of different forces which either trigger it off or stifle it. Within such a mix, different forces, from time to time, play a critical or catalytic role, but this they do always in concert with other forces and not just by themselves. Such a mix of forces, and their specific interaction with one another, in which different forces play the internally critical role in concert with other forces, is rarely emphasised in development studies. This is because of the way social science knowledge has developed, emphasising the importance, or even the exclusivity, of certain powerful factors at the expense of, or even at the negation of, certain other factors. Through its various specialisations, extolling the factors that its branches are interested in, it has then extended into development studies its own monocausal emphasis on behalf of those factors. Consequently, what we often end up knowing about development process is what economics or political science or (to a lesser degree) anthropology wants to tell us, in isolation of other disciplines. In their present form, or in the manner of their current extensions into development studies, these separate specialist branches of knowledge do not help us to cultivate the necessary sensitivity, let alone understanding, of the *interaction* of various forces in the development process.

Moreover, even within such a select approach, we are inclined to argue about the development process with the help of a group of postulates, and then build a chain of deductive reasoning based on them. More often than not, we tend to build our own postulational systems, and even before checking them out with reference to actual situations where the development process is sought to be examined, we come up with our own chain of deductive inferences.

A generation of social scientists who came under the influence of social science methodology, which in turn was, directly or indirectly, influenced by Karl Popper's view on the impossibility of inductive knowledge, found itself much at ease with an intellectual exercise involving movement from assumptions or postulates and their deductions to a groping approximation of social reality, rather than, from time to time, checking out the tenability and effectiveness of those postulates by means of challenges to them in real situations. But somewhere a place must be given to inductive inferences derived from those situations so that the validity of your assumptions may be checked.

To field work social scientists, and to students of development studies in particular, Karl Popper's legacy of denying the very possibility of inductive knowledge or even its secondary or tertiary role – whereby one approaches the existential situation not with a blank mind, but with rival or counter hypotheses sustained by data collected for the testing of previous hypotheses – has not been very helpful. For he has given an added justification, as it were, despite his acknowledged *ethic of falsifiability*, to the notion of the futility of wanting to know more than one's initial postulates and assumptions, by discovering challenges to them in the very process of empirical and existential research. The point in question here is whether the data collected to test a hypothesis, which did not make the grade, can be used to find out what else it will sustain by way of another hypothesis. That then forces us to take the existential situation more seriously.[1]

But even when we break out of the Popperian influence, known or unknown, to get a first-hand look at the reality, we rarely repeat the kind of cognitive exercises that were undertaken by Albert Hirschman, and in which anthropologists engage all the time, of going back to the source of what we theorised about. Most of us build our case with the help of government-supplied reports and figures, or surveys done by professional agencies, or send our needy research students to 'find out' for us what the development process and its complexity are all about. And in all this, the research personnel involved is almost always a social science discipline trained individual looking at the problems of development through the segmented perspectives of his or her discipline.

Since the development process is rarely characterised as a product of the *interaction* of various forces, the capability of the various concepts and theories used in development studies, to identify, explain, and even measure the consequences of such interactions is neither developed nor refined from time to time in the light of perceived inadequacies. Consequently, conceptually speaking, in development studies we are still at ground zero. We have yet to recognise the inadequacy of our fragmented social science specialisations and theories, and the near-total absence of a body of conceptual knowledge which can do justice to the phenomenon of development, which has interaction of forces at its root. Only after such a recognition can we begin our exploratory attempts at building, incrementally, the much-needed body of knowledge which may be able to address itself to the peculiar problems of development, rather than live on the intellectual capital provided by the social sciences.

Within the social sciences we are far more comfortable with institutions and policies, on the one hand, and the way groups and individuals behave, on the other. But we are not all comfortable with the problem of identification of the social and political *process*. Since processes are always dynamic, fluid and unsettled, we cannot be sure that we can always identify them with certainty. Consequently, barring some bold scholars, who would go out no matter where their problems take them, the general tendency is to avoid any discussion of process, and to be content with what is settled or institutionalised. Once you can identify what is institutionalised, you can then take the next respectable, and even scientific, step of 'classification'. And even if the process-obsessed scholars say that your 'classification' is merely another name for 'petrification', you may not want to give up the intellectual security provided by its anchor in an uncharted sea of processes.[2]

It is said that a quarter of a century ago, the biological sciences were in a similar predicament. The classificatory categories had stifled any scope for either moving into new regions or identifying the more intellectually challenging areas of biological processes. But biology came out with sufficient scientific daring to go into new fields such as biochemistry and biotechnology, on the one hand, and biological process, on the other.[3]

A similar cognitive daring now awaits development studies, so that it can reveal its processes, which have been excluded from their purview because of the limitations of the social sciences on which we totally depend. Such an exercise, at comprehension of the development process, would require a far deeper understanding of how development actually takes place, or does not, in the presence of certain stimuli or initiatives. Such an intellectual assault would then help us to probe deeper into empirically identifiable processes – unencumbered by the reductionist biases implicit in social science-embedded approaches.

Such an attempt at identifying the development process implies that in our fresh round of cognitive effort, we would also be engaged in carving out an area of intellectual inquiry which is to be looked at differently from anything before. The earlier development studies were segmented on the lines of the disciplines, and within those they were guided by the identification of discrete variables in isolation of others. We grouped together such variables when our inquiry so demanded, but rarely in their interactive relationships so as to get at the *process* of development. Thus rather than studying chopped-up development phenomena with the help of equally disparate variables (as we did previously), what we shall be required to do is to get a conceptual grasp on the notions of development processes, as they become increasingly clear to us in our efforts at probing them. And unlike the previous approaches, with their assurances of 'conclusive' understanding of the complexity of the development process, the new approach will for ever keep us on our intellectual and conceptual toes, requiring constant probing into the deeper layers of the development experience, and a constant refinement of our conceptual formulations so that we may understand those layers.

Such a renewed intellectual attempt at development studies would also require a deeper understanding of the *society* within which the development process is to be studied. The studies of society by sociologists in 1950s and 1960s, and the various theories which they formulated, were deeply rooted in their own understanding of Western societies and, to that extent, were highly ethnocentric. Today, with greater awareness of the fact of diversity among societies, such intellectual efforts should not miss out on the essential plurality of social systems. Against the background of such studies we can then examine the nature of the continuum which a variety of development efforts entail.

Our intensive examination of the development continuum should then help us to identify, and manipulate through interventionist efforts, the forces which are interactive, sequential, mutually reinforcing or competitive, countervailing or effective in the short run – and so on. Simultaneously, we should be able to gauge the effectiveness of various kinds of interventions or initiatives and identify what they actually do to the development continuum, either by themselves or as co-ordinates of the development process in general.

As illustrations of the development continuum we can briefly look again at the four development initiatives, and their social consequences, that we analysed in Chapter 3. The many-sided public initiatives which had sought to reorganise economic, political and social institutions of free India at the grassroots level, triggered off responses from various segments of her society whereby those with the traditional social and economic advantages over others got much more out of those initiatives than did the rest. The broader incorporation process set in motion by various public initiatives could not get past the antecedent social inequality of India's traditional organisation and ended up by getting unequal responses to the various opportunities meant to be equally available to everyone.

Such an initial advantage for some was strengthened by various individual economic initiatives whereby the very nature of traditional occupations favoured those in the upper echelons of India's hierarchical society. The castes with greater potential for economic growth were precisely those whose traditional occupations, with improved and innovated skills, were also likely to benefit the most by the opportunities provided by development stimuli. Conversely, those in traditional occupations, whose skills were not much in demand in the general thrust for development, were the least likely to benefit by development stimuli.

Even in the co-operative initiative this advantage in the development process reappeared. It was an initiative which had philosophical sympathies for the less well off. But there too, as we saw in Chapter 3, the better off got more out of it. While some found their economic prospects in it, such as the animal breeding caste of the Chaudhuries, others, such as the Kshatriyas, waited to be led by their own ethnic leaders.

The development continuum that we examined earlier also showed that in an unequal society the providing of new economic opportunities to some of its economically backward segments was not enough. They needed to be helped, in addition, at least initially, by a human agency. Only when such an intermediary was present, which was also interested in their self-development through self-involvement, did they respond to the development opportunity in a comprehensive fashion.

Chapter 3 thus revealed many complex patterns of development continuum, and their social consequences, not all of which were going in the intended direction.

This then takes us to the wider significance of the development process and the need for manipulation of it in accordance with our vision and the goal that it must serve. The entire exercise of getting a firm grip on the development process has to be conceived against the background of 'development for what?'. We shall examine that in the next section on the development core.

III   THE DEVELOPMENT CORE

Let us now briefly identify some of the issues which could be regarded as the *core* issues in development, at least in those emerging societies which, because of a variety of social and historical reasons, have a high degree of social inequality. In addition to their economic backwardness, which always receives maximum attention, we also need to look at the nature of social inequality in those societies which, in a significant way, contributes to their all-round underdevelopment. In order to undertake such an exercise, we shall have to identify those core issues which must be integral parts of development goals across the disciplinary divides of the social sciences. Moreover, to be realistic in our formulation of those issues, we shall have to extrapolate them from the development experiences of any specific society or societies, to begin with, and then make such an understanding the basis of a wider theoretical argument with significance for other societies.

At the heart of those core issues, whether in social, political or economic development, is the *human factor*. The social sciences in their anxiety to be 'scientific' or 'objective' have increasingly settled for positivist positions and thereby ignored the consequences of the rest on the human estate. An examination of the human factor, which is at the centre of core issues in development, will be briefly undertaken in this section, and the theoretical significance of such an approach will be taken up in the following section, on *ethnodevelopment*.

All developing societies – for reasons of their internal social organisations, traditions of authoritarian rule, religion-supported civil or military autocracies, colonialism or colonial intrusion – manifest a lack of human capacity to secure a responsive and accountable government under the rule of law. The problem of the growth of human capacity to secure this, therefore, should constitute a core issue in development. For such an ungrown or limited or crippled human capacity also results in an uneven economic development of the various segments of those societies. Consequently, the problem of human capacity, *vis-à-vis* institutions, decision-makers, economic unequals or social superiors, is not merely a political problem. It is in fact a many-sided problem with significance for many fields.[4]

Most of the social and economic theories which we have in the social sciences – which are themselves rooted in the social and historical experiences of a few industrialised societies where, relatively speaking, more balanced social development has taken place – miss out on the core issues, such as human development, which are central to developing societies. Consequently, any discussion of core issues must rest on what the developing societies have *actually* experienced, both socially and historically.

Scholars doing field research in developing countries, in rural or urban communities, become acutely aware not only of the forces of culture and traditional social organisation but also of what these have actually done to the various segments of people in those societies. The differences among the various segments, as the scholars also become aware, are then further reinforced by a network of economic and political relationships. What thus stands out is the wide difference among the segments, in their relative capacity, as people. Such a difference in human capacity then registers a differentiated response even to a uniform development stimulus or a participatory opportunity. Neither our social science theories, nor indeed development theories, have so far shown enough sensitivity to the problem of human inequality in emerging societies. Some of the socially disadvantaged there are unable to benefit even from the opportunities especially created for them. The presumption of our theories has always been that once you create an opportunity, or provide an institutional facility, the disadvantaged and the unequal will come out with adequate responses to them. Such has been the assumption of a variety of rational choice theories in economics and politics which are based on the nineteenth- and twentieth-century, relatively homogenised and socially equalised Western industrial societies. This assumption is now being challenged even in industrialised societies, however, by women, ethnic groups, immigrants and guestworkers.

However, in the context of the emerging countries, the problem of social inequality is still more pronounced. There even the very notion of 'equal opportunity' does not give the true picture: of human beings who are unequal because of the deeply institutionalised social inequality in their traditional social organisation; of cultural values forcing people to come to terms with whatever they have; and of a crippled political capacity, by which they are unable to benefit from the opportunities created for them by socially concerned public policy. Those we are referring to here are not less capable human beings as such, but some among them made so by various social and traditional constraints, making them also unequal utilisers of opportunities specially created for them. We illustrated this with reference to the tribals and the untouchables of rural India. In our general discussion on the development core, therefore, we must not lose sight of the fact of the deeply rooted social inequalities, some of which cannot be overcome by means of mere provisions of public policy or participatory opportunity.

In a manner of speaking, the core issues often crystallise within the cumulative experiences of the development process of any particular society. Consequently, a number of development policies, which were based on the experiences of advanced industrial societies, failed to address themselves to the pressing issues in developing societies. In that respect the failed development efforts, which were based on prescriptions derived from Western development experience, have also become a relevant source of guidance on what else needs to be emphasised in any specific developing society.

Such was the significance of the development experience of India in the field of the democratisation of her decision-making institutions, at all levels of government, and of making them responsible and accountable to the electorate.

For the founding fathers of Indian republic, the core issue of establishing political democracy, based on the principle of universal suffrage, freedom to question and hold the executive responsible for its actions, a bill of rights and an independent judiciary to protect it, and so on, came from the prior commitment of the nationalist leaders who were fighting for independence from alien rule. For such a purpose, up to a point, they could also make use of the age-old participatory *panchayats*, local councils, which had survived through India's long and chequered history, by revamping them with the help of universal adult suffrage. But the hope of the founding fathers of India's liberal political institutions was that the mere presence of such institutions would stimulate effective political drives in all the segments of her hierarchically ordered society, enabling the lower segments to circumvent the disadvantages imposed on them, and from there, to build a new political society which would gradually erode the age-old fortress of traditional privilege based on social and economic status. This hope did not fully materialise. The democratic momentum which was supposed to shake up and reshuffle social and economic positions, fell short of what it was expected to do. While it materially altered political relationships between various strata of society among the top two-thirds of its constituents, it did not make any appreciable change in the economic and social status, or indeed political effectiveness, of the lowest one-third where the disadvantaged and the deprived are concentrated.

In other words, the newly introduced democratic process, in its encounter with the traditional society, could retain its edge and effectiveness in that component of society where various hierarchically ordered segments were capable of responding to an external stimulus or development opportunity. It was effective in those segments whose mobility and capability to pursue such an opportunity had not been drained out of them, despite the cultural values favouring the elderly and those with higher social status. Consequently, four decades of democratic process saw much mobility, both political and economic, among such segments of society. And whenever some of the segments, especially among the middle castes, held themselves back from involvement in the participatory process, it was due to a lack of the role model for such an involvement from one of their own.

Within the rural communities throughout India, one could notice the shift of political power from the Brahmins and the upper caste Rajputs, who had previously combined social status with economic resources, to the various argriculturist castes traditionally lower than them in social status. But the same democratic process, despite formal equality before the law and in voting rights, and despite a number of affirmative actions in social policy, and, above all, despite the numerical strength of the poor – a solid one-third segment of society – could do precious little to stir them up to claim all that was promised by the institutional provisions.

The lowest one-third segment, apart from being economically dependent on landowners with larger tracts of land, was also the segment which was almost untouched by the mass movement launched by Mahatma Gandhi during the national independence movement, and remained little affected by the continued democratic ferment of elections at the five different levels of authority, namely village, sub-district, district, state, and union. The upper two-thirds segment, because of its exposure to the national movement and later on to the democratic process, has cumulatively built its political capacity to transact its business with public officials. This segment went from strength to strength in building its own political effectiveness. As compared to the politically initiated two-thirds, however, the lower one-third did not even build enough political capacity to become the demanders and takers of what was provided for then in public policy.

The budgetary provisions made for the lower one-third segment of Indian society, in one five-year plan after another, went directly or indirectly to those who needed them the least. No matter for whom the development goodies were meant, they always ended up with the most prosperous.

The newly introduced democratic political institutions thus did not automatically help India's most needy and helpless. On the contrary those people were short changed even in provisions which were explicitly made to enhance their own economic well-being. From the point of view of our discussion on core issues, the significance of such an unequal development outcome was enormous.

Through various stages of India's social history, saints, sages, religious protests and social reform movements, the national movement for independence with its enormous emphasis on constructive programmes, and, above all, the various provisions of the constitution of free India and public policy, all of these have tried to involve the people themselves in building a new society. But the lowest one-third segment have missed out on all those opportunities because they were not considered to be an integral part of society. Consequently, throughout her history, the poor were left out and as such they had to appeal to the sense of fairness and moral obligation of the better off, and the government of the day, to act as the guardians of their welfare. This segment, therefore, did not emerge, as described earlier, as the demanders and takers of what they were entitled to, but always depended on the better off, or the higher up, to favour it with merciful dispensations.

The lesson of the impenetrability of specific kinds of human social barriers, and the consequent inability of certain segments to make use of the participatory provisions effectively – something experienced in all societies, either by indigenous groups or by immigrants who came later – is repeatedly lost on the theorists of social and political development. For they often take for granted an equal human political capacity, at all levels, to use the various participatory provisions of society. Such theories were formulated in Western societies, which had already acquired, through their gradual process of social evolution, education, urbanisation and modernisation, a much greater degree of equality of political capacity. In our examination of the core issues in development we therefore need to take a hard look at those theories which assume an antecedent social homogeneity and social equality in all societies.[5]

Moreover, even in the top two-thirds, the democratic process, instead of incorporating the existing society – providing various segments in it with new goals, directions and institutional facilities for their political expressions and drives – reflected, at least initially, the deep disparity within society. However, the reflected picture was not the exact picture. For this time around, the social cohesion and numerical strength of certain caste groups within society also played an important part, by helping them to get new access to political power. Agriculturist castes of medium economic strength, but with numerical superiority, began to play a more effective role in the participatory institutions of rural India. Democratic institutions thus gave facilities to people in the middle rungs of India's hierarchical social organisation to get involved in the political process and thereby develop their own political capacity. The participation of the lower segments in such a process, because of their internal divisions, and unclear political understanding, remained marginal to the democratic system.

But quite apart from such differing political capacity, democracy has placed a special demand on those non-Western countries which wanted to emulate the liberal political ideal. In the bulk of such countries, including Japan, Sri Lanka and India, the primary social experience has been one of associated living. Unlike the countries of the industrialised West, these countries had not gone through a historical experience of individuation. As opposed to that the political societies of Western countries, through the Roman Law, feudalism, Protestant Revolution, theories of social contract and natural rights, the French Revolution, and, above all, the laissez-faire capitalism had been continually exposed to an individualising and atomising process. Such an exposure had brought forward the individual *qua* individual to take on himself/herself the new individualised roles in society, politics and economic matters, and in a large range of other issues. Whether as an individual demanding property or participatory rights, or as a worshipper in church, or indeed as an economic entrepreneur launching economic initiatives, it was always the individual who was in the centre of things.

Consequently, when the developing countries began borrowing or emulating liberal political ideals and institutions from Western societies, they did not realise that they were going to subject their people to two kinds of living: associated living in social life, and individuated living in political life. Since most of the leaders of nationalist movements, and the makers of the constitutions and legal and political institutions were, by and large, lawyers, who were deeply steeped in the Western liberal legal and political ideals, they saw little or no contradiction in what they were doing. And those among them who became aware of the problem tried to convince themselves by saying that in due course the individualised values, borrowed from the West, would permeate all other societies.

So far as Western political societies were concerned, they were not confronted with such a diversity of demands. As stated earlier, their various historical and social experiences had gradually, and over a period of several centuries, moved them in that direction. Moreover, the growth of liberal political institutions along with entrepreneurial capitalism, from the eighteenth century onwards, had prepared those societies, as it were, for the new social and political institutions and the part which individuals *qua* individuals were going to play in them.

In contrast, those developing societies which made a successful switch to liberal democracy, had to go through an experience of workable social dualism which allowed them to retain their associated living in social life and also, simultaneously, transact their political business in participatory democracy as individuals. Such a dualism, for obvious reasons, could not be strictly compartmentalised. The values of associated living continually figured in the operations of the new institutions, either as a need to have the security of primary groups, and their interests, or as a means of tapping the social cohesion of caste groups, for electoral purposes, by turning them into 'vote banks'.

At the level of human political capacity, such a dualism placed some new demands on all segments of society. The individuated response required by the liberal institutions appeared to be more easily obtainable in the upper strata of the traditional society than in the lower. The lower down you went, the more cohesive the social segments became in their political response.

The demand of the new political institutions for an individuated political response, however, had a strange ally in the Indian belief systems, in particular Hinduism. Unlike the traditional social organisation, which underscored group living and compliance in essential caste matters, the Indian belief system had created conditions for the growth of the individual and his/her pursuit of noble ideals, inner experience, and ultimately *mokasha*, all these strictly as an individual, unrelated or untied to anyone else. So the individual trained by the belief system, as it were, proved to be most receptive to the demands of the new political system, which was premised on the assumption that the individual would participate in the new political institutions as an individual, and build and operate secular, political and economic collectivities across ethnic and religious divides. There again, the individualised behaviour inspired by belief systems was more in evidence in the upper strata of society than in the lower.

In terms of the growth of human political capacity, such a social dualism, after an initial groping, settled down to a workable compartmentalisation which was not free from infractions. In its interaction with the democratic process, the cohesion of various castes, after an exploratory extension to non-traditional fields, settled down to what may be described as the primary social concerns of castes, those which ensured their own identity and survival. Such concerns showed in matters relating to endogamy, ritual and pollution. Not all castes could mobilise their traditional social cohesion beyond those matters. The castes in search of higher social status could successfully appeal to their members to keep the internal cohesion intact, for obvious reasons. But whenever those castes were involved in the non-traditional matters of economic and political deals, their cohesion did not last long.[6] For all practical purposes, therefore, the effective traditional social cohesion of most of the castes, had shrunk to the outer limits of their own primary concerns.

Those individuals who began realising the significance and instrumentality of the democratic process to protect and enhance their own interest and the interest of their groups, and who had, therefore, involved themselves in various participatory opportunities, grew in their political capacity.[7] And among those individuals, there were some who realised that the most effective way of getting a response from the democratic system, to protect their interests, was to organise a numerically larger support structure which cut across ethnic and religious divides. Rarely could a numerically large ethnic group turn itself into a political unit beyond constituency politics to get a favourable response. The chances of such an ethnic group were better when it aligned itself to a larger secular group.

But in all this the poor, who needed an effective economic and political grouping of their own, did not get round to building it, except in some select regions. Nor did their political capacity become effective enough to get responses from the decision-makers on problems which needed immediate attention. In that respect the poor almost always became somebody else's ward.

A longitudinal study of Anand, a middle-sized town in western

India, which was considered to be politically active, revealed that the bulk of the people there were unable to connect their political power to vote with the electing of deputies who would solve their economic problems.[8] They felt that the public officials, elected or appointed, either dodged or wriggled out of their responsibility. In other words, they had not developed the commensurate political capacity to hold their elected deputies responsible for their performance after the election. Consequently, while there was support for democratic institutions, right across the social spectrum, there was also the frustrating incapacity to hold the elected deputies responsible and accountable.

One of the puzzling questions for students of the social sciences in general, and political development in particular, is why the poor in India, who constitute the world's largest pool of poor, did not develop their political effectiveness over the years, and more specifically during the last four decades of the operation of democratic institutions, and thus make some difference to their own economic condition. Karl Marx, who was deeply sympathetic to the Indians under the British, had hoped that the alien rule would do away with the vertical division of caste and horizontal division of village sentiment. Once that was done, the poor in India, with their deep sense of economic injustice and social indignity, would acquire the much-needed political effectiveness. Nothing of the kind happened. When colonial rule ended, the caste system was in mint condition. It had become even more consolidated on horizontal lines during the *pax Britannica*.[9]

Since then a controversy has persisted among the social scientists on how to view caste as a unit of social analysis, especially as there is nothing comparable to it in the Western historical and social experience. Max Weber, who was always careful in qualifying Western concepts, described caste as ethnicity plus hierarchy and was still not happy with that.[10] Others tried to view it as class, or pre-class or even lumped it together with other income groups.

Underneath such broad and unqualified characterisations, there was also the inability to grasp the actualities of the wider cultural and economic contexts which surround the lower castes, especially their many-sided incapacities, which have trapped them into economically and socially lower level conditions.

The poor in India are not merely economically deprived, but also socially denigrated for being of low caste or belonging to untouchable or tribal groups, and are politically incapable of fighting their way out of their many-sided disadvantages. Such a range of deprivational actualities calls for a far more inclusive approach than we are used to in the social sciences, which have incorporated the social experiences of Western societies. Our examination of the poor in India calls for an approach which questions how economic backwardness, low social status, political incapacity, and the cultural factor of *karmic* rationale, reinforce one another; and how the result of all these, and not of any single factor in isolation of the others, has created a prolonged situation of human helplessness, for which, to date, there is no solution in sight.

In a longitudinal study, spread over nearly two decades, of the four districts in western India where milk co-operative dairying is a phenomenal success, the authors came to the conclusion, as we noted in Chapter 3 (in the sub-section on human self-rebuilding initiative), that what helped some of the poor the most was their own involvement in various situations leading to their own development and to the changing of the many-sided conditions stacked up against them.[11] The study made clear that nothing could shorten the social and political distance between the poor and their traditional superiors – certainly not economic growth in isolation of other conditions, as the Venkars of Gujarat,[12] the Nonias of UP,[13] and the Untouchable brewers of Orissa[14] found out – as effectively as their own involvement in participatory opportunities provided in the various recently established economic and political institutions. Such involvement helped them to shorten the distance between themselves and their traditional superiors. It was also clear that the unfavourable social, economic and political conditions of the past had interrupted their growth as human beings and had placed them as wards at the mercy of others. As opposed to that they had now to become demanders and takers like any other individuals of a free society. In that respect, the poor in India have quite a lot of belated social and political growing up to do. Through their self-involvement, not only can the poor become the effective users of what is already provided for them in various rural policies but they can also force the hands of the decision-makers of the planned economy to make greater provision for their development. For all this the starting point is their own self-involvement.

What is more, such involvement in the participatory process is likely to bring the fellow poor closer, across the ethnic divide, and thereby enhance their own effectiveness. Previously the poor of one ethnic group had thought little of those of other ethnic groups. In a curious situation of vertical economic ties, they had even preferred to have contacts, however limited, with their social superiors, some of whom might have given them a raw economic deal in the past. The operation of the hierarchical principle had, for centuries, conditioned poor to look up to the upper castes, as masters and models to revere and envy, but not to show the open insolence of wanting to be like them. In the traditional world, where each person was equipped with his own flow chart of destiny, that could never be. Only from a distance could one envy and admire, and hope that one's children, with education and better opportunities, would be able to transcend one's own limitations. With all that, the poor, till recently, did not look at the fellow poor across the caste barrier, as a potential source of numerical strength to back up their demands. Instead, in the hierarchical pecking order, they too wanted to be unkind to those of their fellow poor whose traditional social status was not as good as theirs.

In one rural community after another one is amazed to see how even the various segments of the untouchables cannot come together. The Venkars, or weavers, who came to be classed as untouchables because they made use of animal gut for weaving in the past, did not come to terms with such a characterisation and repeatedly complained of deep social injustice done to them by the higher castes, especially the Brahmins. In order to get out of their economic backwardness and social injustice, they worked very hard, put enormous emphasis on education, sent their children to urban centres for employment, and tried to increase their investment in land and milch animals. In a number of villages their standard of education was better than that of the upper castes, with maximum number of newspapers and transistors per capita in the district. But the same Venkars, being at the top of the untouchable pile, will have nothing to do with other untouchables. In fact their prejudice towards other untouchables was probably stronger than anyone else's.

Next within the untouchable hierarchy come the Chamars, or those who deal in animal skins, making shoes and sandals, and earning a living either as tradesmen or craftsmen. Economically some of them have done fairly well, but they are, by and large, indifferent towards the Venkars as well as those below them.

Below Chamars come the Dheds, who are the skinners of dead animals. The Chamars will not socialise with them but only maintain an economic relationship with them.

Last come the Bhangis who are the toilet cleaners and are therefore the lowest of the low. Neither the Venkars, nor Chamars, nor Dheds will have a social relationship with them. In the villages of Gujarat, even those who do the priestly work for each of them, and go from village to village, are different. It would be difficult to come up with another traditional social organisation in the world which is so much divided.

Each of these social segments, continually in search of higher social status – through means such as hard work, economic development, education, urban migration or even embracing Christianity – wishes to avoid any further stigma for having associated with lower castes. The undying hope of improving their social status puts further constraints on their scope for concerted action *as* poor. Even when some of them embrace Christianity, they carry with them the hierarchical grading of the social group from which they came. So even as Christians they invariably fail to generate effective concerted action. Instead they remain content with any educational and employment opportunity that their conversion may bring.

The mere economic poverty of the poor has thus not brought them together. What *is* beginning to bring them together is their involvement in participatory situations where they discover the potential help they can receive from the fellow poor. In such a situation the poor also develop tolerance and a perception of common problems requiring concerted action. Both Mahatma Gandhi and JP understood this and therefore throughout their work among the poor they emphasised their own involvement in their self-development. Thus the poor in a traditional society, they said, had to overcome constraints, barriers and distances through their self-involvement, and so enhance their own political capacity, self-esteem, and human potential.

The students of the social sciences have yet to appreciate, fully, the complex and many-sided nature of poverty and underdevelopment in the lower strata of different societies. So far we have taken the case of India where a mere economic characterisation of the problem of the poor limits and even distorts their many-sided problems. In other developing societies too one may discover an equally complex problem of the poor. And in each case the human capacity to grow out of those conditions will require an understanding of the actual nature of the constraints of the poor, and not guesswork with the help of prematurely formulated theories claiming universal validity.

All developing societies – due to their prolonged history of arbitrary rule, or peculiar conditions created by the nature of their traditional social organisation, belief system, and/or Western colonial intrusion – have had, by definition, an abnormal and interrupted social and political growth. Such a growth often influenced people to subscribe, in an unqualified manner, to the social and political demands of the primary groups to which they were born. And such groups, in return, gave to their constituents that sense of security which comes out of shared values and concerns. But when such primary groups and shared values were superseded in specific areas, by the emergence of a wider political society, as a result of the introduction of the new liberal legal and political institutions, and the participatory opportunities provided by them, people were forced to subscribe to new or additional set of values, along with others who did not belong to their primary group. In such circumstances, one retains the wider social and religious values of one's primary group, and also, side by side, subscribes to some of the commonly shared values which underlie the new political institutions and practices. Such new values should either be able to strike roots in the indigenous ethical traditions or appear parallel to them, or else they will remain on an infirm footing.

In most developing societies the élites in various walks of life have sought to 'root' the new values in the indigenous ethical traditions either by pointing out the desirability of their inclusion or by indicating strands parallel to them in the indigenous.

But in order to be politically effective, it is necessary not only to have values – indigenous, borrowed or indigenised – but also to pursue them in concert with others. In other words, the citizens of developing societies are required to develop a human capacity for normative–pragmatic balance, which keeps them hinged to their normative commitments, and at the same time induces them to learn the necessary political skill, and effective use of means, to realise them in practice. The idea then is to learn to moderate the extremes of the normative values of one's group, or ideologies, or personal commitments, so as to make those values realisable, in concert with others, in social and political life. At the same time one cannot shed all one's normative commitments in search of an overly pragmatic approach. One learns to strike such a normative–pragmatic balance in what I have called elsewhere *political society*, which allows you to subscribe to your primary group values in your broader social and cultural life, but at the same time persuades you to strike a balance between your broader normative commitments and the search for pragmatic means which remain within the bounds of legality, propriety, and morality.

Political society thus represents an arena where one does one's necessary political growing up learning to operate the new liberal political institutions, balancing one's normative considerations with the pragmatic, with individuals who do not belong to one's primary group. It is also an arena where one learns that the pursuit of the zero-sum game, for which there is constant temptation, has its own chain reaction often boomeranging on oneself.

Through one's political growing up one is able to make up for either an unhelpful historical social and political condition or colonial intrusion which has interrupted one's normal growth. Such political growing up is essential, and possible only through self-involvement in a participatory process.

In all political societies, developed or developing, individuals are constantly required to do their additional political growing up in the face of new challenges and constantly changing nature of such societies. Technological developments, the ever increasing sophistication of the media and their manipulators, and the ever-changing nature of political relationships have posed, from time to time, different kinds of challenges for our own political growth. In that respect the people of developing countries have a lot of political growing up and catching up to do. Whether in the developed or in the developing societies, political growing up has now become an unceasing requirement.[15]

This then brings us to the core issue in development, namely the development of human capabilities to meet the challenges of a delayed economic or political development. That is to say we need to view the problem of development from a much more inclusive approach. To that we now turn.

IV   ETHNODEVELOPMENT

It is evident from the foregoing section that at the heart of development issues is the core issue of human development. I have chosen to call it *ethnodevelopment* or the development of many-sided human capacities. Those capacities have to be pulled out of their manifold constraints of underdevelopment, and regenerated. The more under-developed and unequal the society, the more complex are the imperatives of ethnodevelopment within it.

Apart from the fact that most developing societies have had historical setbacks in their normal historical development, and uninterrupted growth, because of either internal or external reasons, they have almost always had an additional internal problem of unequal growth of various social segments within them. Consequently, economically as well as politically, the various segments benefit unequally from either development stimuli or affirmative actions which seek to target them for an accelerated pace of development. This forces us to probe deeper into the problem of human capacity/incapacity to benefit from the various provisions of institution and policy. Any examination of development effort and response, therefore, ought to take us from the economic stimuli, institutional provisions, policies, and so on, to the human responses to them which, in most emerging societies, are unequal. Consequently, any search for the core issues in development inevitably brings us to the core of core issues, namely, the human capacity to respond to development stimuli.

Behind the unequal human capacity to benefit from development stimuli lie the unequal social segments and the peculiar network of social relationships, which have imposed certain constraints and disadvantages on some of those segments. Consequently it is not enough to talk about development as a stimulus from the top or the outside. It is equally necessary to find out what happens to development stimuli in terms of the actualities of human responses to them. It is with such a purpose in mind that we took a detailed look at the development process from a grassroots perspective, so as to gain a clearer understanding of the nature of differentiated response to development stimuli in a society with deeply institutionalised inequalities.

In Chapter 3, in the section on human self-rebuilding initiatives, we also saw the need for a human agency, over and above institutional opportunities and policy provisions, to involve most of the economically depressed and those with the lowest social status in development opportunities. In the case of the milk co-operatives of Western India, the social and political capacity of the tribals and various other backward social segments was not developed enough to respond directly, and without the aid of a human intermediary (at least initially), to development stimuli.

So far most of our studies of the poor in developing societies have been in terms of their economic deprivation. What almost all of them have done is to abstract poverty from the poor so that it can be 'scientifically' identified and then measured. Once you identify poverty you can then apply abstract, and postulate-deduced, intellectual propositions, and then presume the correspondence between such propositions and the actualities of poverty.

What is, nevertheless, forgotten in such 'scientific' treatment of poverty is that there is much more to the poor than their economic poverty. In India for example, in addition to their economic deprivation, there is also the deeply internalised sense of marginality – as almost all the poor are of lower castes, untouchables, and tribals – which the rigidly hierarchically ordered social organisation of their country has inculcated. Such a sense of marginality is further reinforced by means of the load of semi-religious mythologies which induce the poor to accept their positions of exclusion, deprivation, and secondariness on the grounds of past deeds. Given such a background, the poor in India do not even think of using the participatory opportunities in the new political system, and economic institutions such as the milk co-operatives, on their own. They need some mobilising human agencies to exhort them and take them to those opportunities, at least initially, till they begin to connect their self-involvement in those participatory opportunities with the possibility of economic improvement in their condition.[16]

What this boils down to is that for the purposes of development studies we need to go away from the notion of a block of people stricken by poverty, to the poor in any particular society, to get a clear perception of the range of their actual disadvantages – the economic reinforced by the social and political. In other words, we need to go beyond the objective disadvantages of the poor to their actual human disabilities.

Later on we shall see how the above position forces us to go back to the contexts of poverty. Our social science theories, as they have developed, have reduced specific existential problems to abstractions for the sake of objective and scientific treatment. And that has been fruitful in a number of fields where such isolation and specificity did not do violence to the actual nature of the problem. But such an isolating of the related existential factors in development studies has often distorted our grasp of certain core issues in the field.

In development studies, however, we need to shift back from

the abstractly stated disadvantages of poverty to the actual human disabilities of the poor. So far we have not recognised this as an issue at the very heart of development issues because the social sciences from which we borrow most of our perspectives and conceptual tools for development studies have themselves not shown any interest in those disabilities.

The question of ethnocapacity, or the social and political capacity, especially of the disadvantaged in the hierarchically ordered society of India, becomes the central issue because the poor have failed to benefit significantly from the planned development efforts of the last four decades, which ostensibly targeted them. It then dawned on perceptive field researchers and scholars that in the poor they were also dealing with a people whose human capacity to benefit from various development efforts was itself crippled. In a sense their prolonged condition of economic disadvantage and social denigration, since the dawn of Indian civilisation, had robbed them not only of their essential human dignity but had also diminished them as people. An extra effort – not only in terms of affirmative action, with special policy provisions, but also one in which human beings helped out other human beings who were emerging from a prolonged state of disadvantage and diminution – was needed.

But there again one could commit the mistake of treating the poor as wards of bureaucrats or of social workers, especially when affirmative action was proposed, for an overly prolonged period of time. In either case there was the risk of unwittingly introducing development paternalism, and thereby once again depriving the people intended to be helped of their own opportunity for self-development through self-involvement. Those who need the extra help, need it only for an initial period. After that the growth of their human capacity should come through their own involvement in participatory processes. The idea is to make their capacities grow so that they can then take care of themselves and not continue to treat their helpers, either bureaucrats or social workers, as crutches.

Such an interpretation of ethnodevelopment highlights the responsibility for the development of the poor on the élites and social workers of every developing country. For too long they have sought solutions of the problem of uneven development through government agencies, bureaucrats and external aids. While all these have a place in a number of areas of development, they have not produced significant results in precisely those segments of society in developing countries where effective development efforts are urgently needed. Whatever may be the truth of the trickle-down theory, what specific developing countries need, so far as their poorer segments are concerned, is a massive internal effort to help build in their own disadvantaged groups the necessary human social and political capacity to stand on their own. After that those groups would stand in a similar development-response situation as the others.

V   BACK TO THE CONCEPTUAL DRAWING BOARD

To go back to the conceptual drawing board, as it were, we need to know what specific problems we ought to be addressing in our renewed round of cognitive effort, so as to build or rebuild, incrementally, a corpus of theoretical knowledge which, after the initial flashes of intuitive projections, and deductions from assumptions, is firmly rooted in the actualities of development experiences of emerging countries. We now need to add an inductive component, based on those experiences, to our existing body of theoretical ideas, which are based almost entirely in the development experiences of Western countries. For too long, we have moved in one direction only: from the theories rooted in Western experiences of development, and at best a few newly postulated theories, and policies deduced therefrom. The time has now come to extend our cognitive efforts to the understanding of the actual consequences of those policies and the development experiences that they generated, and to go on from there to the exploration of the significance of such experiences for the refinement and reformulation of our theoretical knowledge. To undertake this fresh round of cognitive effort we need to address ourselves to the following four points: (a) the irreversibility of segmented theories, (b) premature attempts at development theory construction, (c) recognition of the primacy of development experience, and (d) an inclusive and incremental effort at development theory construction. Let us now examine each of these in some detail.

(a) The Irreversibility of Segmented Theories

As stated earlier, development studies under the influence of the social sciences have come to acquire a disciplinary orientation. Such an orientation has also led to the formulation of a body of theoretical ideas which is sensitive and responsive to particular kinds of problems raised in those disciplines. Consequently, we often get only a sliced-up perspective on problems of common concern to those disciplines. Under these circumstances even a unified social science perspective on those problems, let alone a development studies perspective, is hard to come by. As observed earlier several branches of the social sciences have neatly carved out an area for themselves and have in effect annexed chunks of development studies territory to their own. Such annexations have taken place in economics, political science, sociology, anthropology and other related disciplines. And there seems to be hardly any discussion on what in fact is the residual territory of development studies.

Within the various disciplinary approaches to development studies, what has reinforced their mutual isolation, as we saw earlier, is the body of theoretical ideas with its own intellectual respectability for the pursuit of specific problems in its own distinctive fashion.

Then there are the vested interests which have developed round each of the specific approaches to development studies. There is the continuous flow of funds for research, travel abroad, consultancies and the like, with not always stringent standards applied for the evaluation of work done. Consequently, there is little willingness to break out into new areas and face the uncertain future. Prudence, therefore, lies in not shaking the boat too much. Everybody, so far, has got something out of this business of development.

The disciplinary approach, with its own pay off, fortified by a body of theoretical ideas which has grown round it, makes the segmented approach to development studies almost irreversible. Not only that, academic norms have now grown in each of the disciplinary approaches which tend to run down the intellectual worthwhileness of any interdisciplinary or co-disciplinary approaches.

Consequently, any exploration of development theory construction which aims at being more inclusive, will have to come to terms with the disciplinary approaches which are deeply entrenched in development studies. At the moment the segmented approaches are immutable. The only way to tackle their isolation is not by extolling the virtues of interdisciplinary approaches but by identifying, by means of rigorous field research and adequate theoretical propositions, the problems within development studies which may have escaped their attention and which require approaches beyond the capability of any of the social sciences. And there are plenty of those to identify in the discipline-sliced approaches of the social sciences. Some of them have been identified in this volume.

One dreams of reversing intellectual respectability from the special-ised disciplinary approach to a multi-dimensional approach by means of the sheer quality and perceptiveness of one's research, and then waiting for the intellectual excitement, and persuasion, that it generates among one's fellow scholars. Such an effort could begin, appropriately, in areas of development studies which have hitherto escaped colonisation by disciplinary approaches. From such a residual territory it may be possible, some day, to piece together, or deslice, approaches to development studies which the social sciences have given to us so far.

To undertake such an exercise, especially in establishing a new area in development studies, requiring a more comprehensive approach, beyond the cutting and slicing which go on in disciplinary studies, we need to know the philosophical and methodological significance of other intellectual efforts when faced with corresponding pre-dicaments.

Such an exercise will be frowned upon, denounced as naïve, insolent and a sheer waste of time, and shot at by hitherto superior, and intellectually more respectable, approaches of various disciplines. But what we now need is a paradigm switch in the Kuhnian sense of the term: one which can give us a new perspective on development studies in place of the petrified disciplinary approaches which we have; the identification of exciting problems for research; and a new methodology and approach to studying them.

The existing approaches to development studies set up their own notions of 'objectivity', 'science', 'rigorous approach' and so on, by formulating 'abstractions' so as to identify and measure problems. Such an approach not only limited but also distorted the actualities of various development processes and problems. The greatest victims of such approaches were the intractable, but central, cultural and human factors in development studies. By excluding the human factor, and the human beings in the centre of development process, and also by excluding cultural and normative factors which orient human action, the various discipline-inspired approaches to development studies came out with highly impoverished, and unrealistic, notions of development. Consequently any attempt at formulating fresh propositions for development studies ought to restore the human and the cultural factors.

Furthermore, as we shall see in some detail in this section, instead of facing the realistic challenges of the complexity of development process, the reductionist theories of disciplinary approaches have continually pared off from them what they could not 'fit' into their preformulated and predetermined frameworks. Consequently, instead of making a fresh effort to let theoretical formulations acquire a more inclusive character, by facing the complexity of the development process, what we finally come to have is what those disciplines with their limitations could actually manage.

There is not much that one can do about such disciplinary approaches to development studies. For they continually draw intellectual sustenance from the mainstream social sciences and their theoretical dynamism. What can be done, instead, as stated earlier, is to build, gradually, those areas of development studies where the disciplinary approaches have either not penetrated or where their intellectual performance is the poorest and then piece together one's work in such areas for a more inclusive approach to development studies.

(b) Premature Theory Construction

The conceptualisation in development studies, and in particular in the field of economic growth, since the Second World War, which has been, by and large, an extension of Western economic theory, as Gunnar Myrdal has pointed out, is both inadequate and premature. It failed to grasp the basic fact that economic growth in non-Western societies is not yet delinked from various cultural or 'institutional' factors. Such a conceptualisation also ignored the fact that the non-Western societies have not come through the same historical experience as the Western societies, and that background makes a lot of difference to the development process. The many different cultural contexts and diverse historical experiences of the non-Western societies presented challenges of diversity and plurality for our cognitive efforts which were not squarely faced by the theories of economic growth. Within such theories there is hardly any evidence of pre-theory, pre-conceptual explorations or rigorous field research into development processes, followed by formulation of a development theory based on the understanding of such processes. What we have instead are the deductions from theories of economic growth zeroing on highly specific variables, in non-Western societies, by cutting them loose from their cultural and historical contexts. Such a wrenching out of highly specific variables from their contexts, as we noted earlier, was the outcome of a wider theory culture within which they found an expression.

The theory culture within development studies puts the Western social and historical experience of development in the centre of everything. It is with reference to the Western experience that you evaluate other experiences, or see them as emulating or deviating from the norm set by it. And such a theory culture, in order to protect itself from accusations either of ethnocentricity or limited experience, has also produced theories to defend theories, almost in the form of an infinite regress.

One of its theories to protect theories implies that you have to have universal criteria for truth, canons of reasoning, and determining of truth itself from falsity. After producing such a universalistic argument, it has also presumed that whatever it already has *is* universally true. And if not, then a rival theory, also based on Western experience, in all probability is likely to take its place for an equal assumption of universal validity.

This theory culture received its first jolt at the hands of field researchers in anthropology, and to some extent in political science, who became painfully aware of the Eurocentric or Westernocentric assumptions of many a development theory. Furthermore, such a theory culture did not want to face the nightmarish questions posed by the continuing controversy surrounding the relativism–universalism debate. In fact it has continually sought to evade several vital issues raised by experiences of development in non-Western societies.

So very aggressive, at times, has been the theory culture that it asserted that empirical evidence ought not to be allowed to judge, conclusively, the validity of theoretical claims. Only theory would determine the truth or falsity of another theory; only a rival theory can displace one that is found wanting. In other words one goes from theory to theory, and not through the intermediate stage of empirical evidence against the claims of an existing theory, and then to a stage when scholars with empirical data find another theoretical argument emerging from what they have collected. Any empirical theory, in the sense of a theory that can be sustained by the facts collected in a previous sequence of controversy, was considered to be not as good as one which started off as pure theoretical conjecture, and at a later date was found to have the support of empirical evidence.

The aggressive theory culture permeated textbooks, research training, and standards for evaluating research proposals and manuscripts for publication, discouraging any deviation from the near apriori status of theories based on intuitive assumptions and conjectures.

You therefore had to begin and end with theory of an acceptable kind. It was unacceptable to start with a tentatively drawn conceptual framework to help launch empirical explorations into the terrain of the unknown, then to keep refining various parts of that framework as they were found wanting during actual investigation, and then, finally, to put together the various pieces of that framework which had come through a process of actual testing, in the form of a theoretical argument.

No way. Such a process would smack too much of theory-empirical research ad hocism. Instead you were advised by the imperatives of theory culture to keep on trying series of self-complete theories till you hit upon the right one.

What is assumed in such an exercise is that you *know* the research terrain and the challenges that it springs at you. So you devote all your time to spawning theory after theory, in a wave-after-wave action, till you hit upon the right one. The cognitive effort involved in such an exercise is concerned with the finding of the right theory, rather than simultaneously finding out more about the problems and their hitherto unknown complexities. For it is thought conceivable that with our mathematical and deductivistic reasoning we can formulate theories which will be right before we know much of the problems about which we begin theorising in the first place. Mathematicians often joke about solutions in their possession, in search of problems.

The truth of the matter is that the theory culture has discouraged discussion on the intellectually messy process of formulating theories and simultaneously, and incrementally, finding out more about the problem. It is the simultaneous discovery of the problem by means of hunches, vague intellectual intimations, and ranges of assertions reflecting an increasing degree of confidence in the crystallising position of the researcher, the constant malleability of the pre-theory and, finally, at the end of the messy meandering, a theoretical position which emerges for testing – it is all these adding to our knowledge which is the *raison d'être of* research.

The problem posed by the theory culture can be formulated as follows: is one's research a way to testing one's theory or, simultaneously, also a way of knowing more about the problem? If the latter is a more acceptable proposition, then we need to look seriously at the way in which we allow the theory culture to set intellectual standards for us.

Such a theory culture is particularly hard on scholars from developing countries, with or without training in Western universities. Despite their grave reservations, but in order to look intellectually respectable and also have visits to Western universities, those scholars often go along with the demands of the theory culture, but, in their private conversations, and even in select seminars, they denounce what they are made to do.

The aggressive theory culture has thus discouraged and, from time to time, shut off any discourse on its own inadequacies. Only when some of the scholars from developing countries get themselves intellectually established do they come out with an open expression of the dissatisfaction, much to the surprise and anguish of their fellow Western scholars, against the distorting demands of the theory culture.

One of the most disturbing aspects of the theory culture, which has remained at the root of development studies is the disequation among the scholars which was there during the colonial days. And some scholars from developed countries have walked into it and have inadvertently revived it. With their advanced training, sophisticated methodology, and power to distribute favours in the form of invitations to contribute to journals and volumes, and visit universities abroad, some Western academics have continued the disequation in the world of scholars by means of possible academic favours. Some kind of academic division of labour emerges, with scholars from developing countries considered good enough for collecting data, and those from developed countries in charge of the intellectually superior work of 'theorising'.

And such a scholarly disequation gets all snarled up when we examine the relationships between the expatriate scholars from developing countries working in Western universities, and the Western native born. It is one in which subtle and indirect claims to disequations are resisted and challenged, with the natives and expatriates forming their own working groups and, in the case of the latter, even identities.

The longevity of scholarly disequation is different in different branches of knowledge. Within the social sciences it was first to weaken in economics, and then in anthropology, but in sociology and political science it has continued unabated.

But apart from the problem of scholarly disequation, where points are scored on the grounds of how good you are in 'theory', the predominant theory culture has permitted counter theories as long as they did not break the basic rule: of not questioning the very limitations and inadequacies of the kind of cognitive exercises which it permitted. You can go on producing rival theories and replacing the existing ones as if they were mere cognitive fashions and fads. You can have any particular theory as long as the general academic ambience considers it respectable. But any attempt at raising the basic issue of the insensitivity of the theory to the complexity of the non-Western world, and suggesting it is therefore inadequate or premature, and thereby challenging the very foundation of the universalism on which the theory culture rests, is discouraged, ignored or even frowned upon.

Nor could the theory culture pay attention to the central issue raised by Marx, Weber, Schumpeter, Myrdal, Hoselitz, and Hirschman with regard to the unseparated nature of development phenomena anywhere, and in particular in the developing countries. Instead the discipline-embedded corpus of theoretical ideas was premised on the assumption either that different aspects of development phenomena have, along with the intermingled whole, a component which is clearly identifiable and therefore can be independently studied, or that such a component itself is so basic to the rest that there should be no hesitation in studying it on its own. In the history of economic and political ideas, colossal thinkers have taken such a position and (barring the thinkers identified above) there have been few discussions about it so far as the growth of Western societies is concerned.

But so far as the perception of development phenomena in non-Western societies is concerned, almost every thinker in any of the branches of the social sciences has a nagging feeling that the fact of the matter there is different. And yet given the powerful theory culture, which extends ideas and theories from the Western, development phenomena to the non-Western, almost always without qualifications, very few scholars have the necessary cognitive daring to take on, single handedly, the established tradition, and risk being consigned to an intellectual doghouse. A Weber, Schumpeter, Myrdal, Hoselitz, Hirschman or the like might get away with it, but others have to think twice before going against the intellectual current.

Consequently, the bulk of the dissatisfied put up with often distorted, unrealistic, limited and inadequate studies of developing societies and, in particular, the Asian, where the forces of history, culture, tradition and so on, have left behind sufficient deposits to influence what Max Weber called orientation to economic action.[17]

The quick answer one often gets to questions about the various kinds of development theories is that since they are universally valid, there cannot be a separate 'African' or 'Asian' theory of development, much less an 'African' or 'Asian' truth. The assumption of universal validity in some of those theories is so unshakeable that you cannot separate the questions relating to 'adequacy' from 'geography'. The point at issue here is not the geographical theory of development or truth, but the validity and adequacy of certain theories when they are confronted with culturally very different conditions. Moreover, the whole issue gets clouded when one talks about 'theory' and 'truth' in the same breath, and thereby assumes that the theory one possesses has a corner on reality or truth.

Theory construction in the field of poverty, the most important issue in development studies, is a case in point. Under the compulsions of theory culture, scholars have prematurely abstracted poverty from the poor so as to identify it and then measure it – in other words, to make its treatment 'scientific'. In so doing they have sought to separate economic deprivation from the host of reinforcing factors which keep the poor in the state of poverty in the first place. If you are looking at the poor in India, how can you afford to neglect the fact they also belong to certain specific social groups such as the lower castes, untouchables, and tribals? Moreover, as we saw earlier, these are also the groups, which, more than the others, deeply subscribe to the doctrine of *karma*, which eliminates the blame from the better off and also dodges the issue of the much needed rationale for an adequate social policy. Finally, as we also saw, despite their numbers in a democratic society (where numbers ought to count), their political capacity to become claimants of what is rightfully theirs has never fully crystallised. There must be, therefore, more to their poverty than mere economic deprivation. To say that everything else follows economic deprivation is far too simplistic, for there are other groups and individuals who have hit the poverty level from time to time, and later come up from it. Only the lower strata of traditional Indian society have been there since the dawn of Indian civilisation. Somehow their place in the traditional social organisation and value system must also have had something to do with their poverty, despite the inability of our theories of development to understand this.

The depersonalisation of poverty is thus a case in point. If you study the 'poor' instead of 'poverty', then you must study the social, cultural, and political contexts of the poor, besides the economic. But if you merely want to study 'poverty' as an abstraction, so that you can apply to it the intellectual machinery developed elsewhere, and thus appear scientific and intellectually respectable, then your understanding will remain inadequate. It is a sad commentary on the theory culture, which has so deeply permeated development studies, that its scholarly endeavours have less and less to do with the actualities of the problems of developing countries. For many of its abstractions should have faced the test of explanatory adequacy and, in the event of failure, should have been replaced. Instead, what has happened in development theory is that while more is being found out about the complexity of the development process, the corpus of theoretical knowledge has shown correspondingly less inclination towards its own refinement in the face of new challenges.

While there is an internal dynamism in theories replacing theories, what we also need in development studies is a keener sense of theoretical inadequacy in the face of our increasing knowledge of the complex terrain of the development process in different societies, and then gradually getting down to the task of refinement and reconstruction of theories that we have. Almost all our development theories are based on the social and historical experiences of Western societies. And the more we come to know about non-Western societies the more we need to refine or reformulate the corpus of the existing theoretical knowledge. As of now there is little or no relationship between the scholarly material which communicates to us the actualities of the development process in developing societies, and development theory proper. Two different sets of scholars are in charge of them, with their relationships ranging from scholarly indifference to disdain.

(c) The Primacy of Development Experience

As stated earlier, one of the significant dimensions of development theory is the antecedent development experience of a society. No matter how limited or mixed in terms of success or failure a society's own experience of development effort may be, when probed in all its critical aspects it can be a very useful guide for that society's future development. There are critical factors to explore in both development success and failure. Because such factors are indigenous, understanding them can be of much greater value than prescriptions borrowed from societies which are different in character.

As we saw in Chapter 1 after the Second World War, developing countries became the objects of replicating prescriptions from economically and politically more developed societies. Under this thrust a number of major scholars gleaned out prescriptions from the development experience of the Western societies and made them available to developing countries. But in the ultimate analysis the emerging countries learnt much more from the success or failure of their own antecedent efforts, or from societies which were closer to them in social and cultural composition.

Lord Robbins, as stated earlier, put his finger on the problem when he said that the theories of economics [as well as of development] are essentially 'historico-relative'. And one should also add that they are socio-cultural and human specific.

One has only to look at the wide range of theories of capitalism, from Adam Smith to Karl Marx to Max Weber to Fernand Braudel and Barrington Moore Jr, to get a range of explanations of the critical combination of factors which made the evolution of capitalism possible, and in different forms in different societies. Max Weber, in his writings, spoke of different kinds of capitalisms, Braudel of different rounds of efforts, and Moore of different combinations of historical agents who produced not only different forms of capitalisms but also their corresponding legal and political institutions. What single prescription can we derive from such scholarly writings and give to developing societies, to adopt as a sure panacea for all their problems of economic backwardness and political underdevelopment?

In Chapter 2, we also examined the diversity of development experiences of different regions and societies. Reference to those diverse experiences can be of critical importance to the development of those regions because it enables them to evolve specific policies based on what they have learnt from their past.

Most societies also give rise to certain kinds of problems, as we also saw in Chapter 3, which are unique to them. The antecedent social inequality of India, which is so deeply institutionalised in various facets of her social life, produces different responses to common development stimuli. The cure for that has to come from the Indian ability to learn from that unique problem. No amount of quick fix from outside even from individuals with great credentials, is going to solve that. Similarly, all societies have certain problems which are unique to them. Only the proportion of the unique to the rest of the problems, with possible common solution, may be different.

The point here is that we need to know the specificity of development problems of each society. And the antecedent experience of development effort may reveal much more about that specificity than a prescription from outside. The specificity of development experience, therefore, becomes the vital dimension in explorations of development theory for practical application.

(d) What Does A Return To The Theoretical Drawing Board Entail?

It entails, first of all, the need to identify the specific nature of interrelated factors which create conditions for development, partial development, or non-development.

For too long we have set our sights on a single or isolated factor because we believe it has led to development elsewhere, presumably in the countries of the West. Whatever may have been the case there, we need to approach such a prescription with a view to finding out the variety of interacting factors on which it was based, and assessing whether those factors can be duplicated elsewhere. A careful assessment of the conditions which actually obtain in the society in which the prescription was followed would encourage us either to come up with an additional effort or to give up the idea of replicating it.

Similarly, underdevelopment too is a consequence of many-sided phenomena, as we saw in relation to poverty, which is often mistakenly characterised as economic deprivation only. This book has often referred to its many-sided, reinforcing characteristics. With reference to our present concern, of returning to the theoretical drawing board, we need to identify the functional relationships between the factors which create conditions of development or non-development in specific societies. In this context any theory should be suspect if it either stops at monocausal explanations or identifies merely the static relationships between conditions which may have led to development or otherwise.

As discussed earlier on in this chapter within the group of interrelated factors to be attended to, for combatting specific areas of underdevelopment we need to zero in on the core issues facing each society and, within those, the central issue of what we have described as ethnodevelopment. Practically all developing societies have gone through the historical and social experiences of arbitrary rule, and have within them social and cultural institutions which sustain social inequality. Most of them have also known colonial intrusion, which deprived them of their own opportunity to face the challenges of social and economic reconstruction. Finally, in some of them, in the post-independence period, political elites, with limited political integrity and little hesitation in violating the basic human rights of their own people, have come into power. While all political societies have tried to attend to some of those problems, their responses to economic, political and human development have been different. And responses have also been different in the case of various social segments within each of those societies.

Such differentiated responses to development effort need to be specifically identified with reference to each situation so that any solution or strategy can address itself to specific problems in particular situations. Each society would register its own peculiar problem of economic backwardness, political underdevelopment or social inequality, or even all of them.

The nature of social inequality, to take it as a special example, is different in different developing societies. And it calls for a special degree of sensitivity, to be able to identify its actuality in different societies. In the past most of our development policies and 'solutions', which claimed to have worked wonders elsewhere, came from outside. Behind them was often the weight of scholarship, the accolade of having worked most effectively in industrialised countries, and the support of the well-meaning international development agencies wanting to help.

The point to be made here, without subscribing to the extreme position of suspecting everything that comes from outside, is that the nature of development problems in each society, such as social inequality, are so very particular that any omnibus remedy for them is not likely to work. In this connection, we took the example of Mahatma Gandhi, and the mass mobilisation launched by him during the freedom movement. The mobilisation touched most of the middle class and upper class peasantry and the urban dwellers, and such a mobilised mass of people, through their own self-involvement in the Gandhian political resistance movement, were able to bring about their own political self-development. After that, politically speaking, they were a different people, who had begun to alter power relationships between themselves and their alien rulers. When the post-independence development opportunities came, they grabbed them first through various participatory mechanisms and influence circuits, and substantially improved their economic, political and social position. Since then they continually looked for new opportunities for themselves.

Nearly three decades of Gandhian mobilisation with best of intentions and efforts, failed to reach the lowest one-third of Indian society. After Gandhi very few of his followers kept up the work of involving people themselves in their development. One such person, as we saw in Chapter 3, was JP. But he too could do precious little. Consequently, due to the lack of their own involvement in demanding what they should get, the lowest one-third of the Indians did not emerge into a participant citizenry demanding and taking what was provided for them in planned development and 'socialist' policies. On the contrary, they remained at the mercy of development bureaucrats, wily politicians, and self-serving élites.

In that sense the Indian case of social inequality is unique. It is unique because along with the fact of economic deprivation, there are also the problems of caste, cultural values and last, but not the least, a crippled political capacity. India therefore needs an equally unique development solution. For apart from economic and educational provisions, the Indians would require a mass social movement, internally directed by a vast army of social workers, to help, initially, the disadvantaged to get themselves involved in the processes of development, rather than remaining at the receiving end of budgetary provisions. Since the problem of social inequality is many-sided, the poor in India would require a many-sided solution, starting with building them back as people with social dignity, rights, opportunities, and wants.

If one were to have a closer look at the nature of social inequality in other developing societies, one would come across equally unique instances requiring highly particularistic solutions. Consequently, in our efforts to go back to the drawing board of development theory construction, we need to pay attention to the unique set of core issues for the development of different societies, and within them the issue of what I have called ethnodevelopment.

We often derive policy prescriptions from economically developed societies. After nearly four decades of prescription-making from the Western models, we have now shifted to the more successful economies of Asia Pacific. And in deriving prescriptions for success from the latter, we might be committing yet another round of similar mistakes.

Since each society is unique, the possible triggers of its development are also unique. Most societies have some success stories, and the factors which gave rise to situations which led to success, no matter how very limited, may have much more to teach us than prescriptions from elsewhere. What this boils down to is a plea for the recognition of development pluralism and within each society the specificity of its own development dynamics.

Max Weber, at the end of his career, as we saw earlier, had become deeply aware of the need to keep a firm eye on the variety of historical and social backgrounds, producing a variety of development situations and institutions. But time and time again, he also worked in the reverse direction – finding similarities in close variants – for his theory construction and classification. The ambivalence in Weber's writings is a salutary reminder for the students of development studies who are in a similar dilemma.

All efforts at theory construction must, by their internal compulsion and logic, narrow down the range of instances of social reality so as to fit them into major theoretical arguments that are derived from their observation. From the point of view of such an imperative, too much attention to diversity and plurality becomes a burden, under the weight of which any attempt at theory construction would either dissolve itself or bring in far too many qualifications and thereby deny itself the necessary cogency and simplicity. The question then is whether we can afford to think in terms of many developments and underdevelopments, social inequalities and poverties, development processes, and so on, and thereby sacrifice some of the imperatives of theory constructions which are not comfortable with the fact of plurality and diversity?

Within development studies, those social and political theories which have been extended from various social science disciplines were either not ready or not refined enough to face the task of recognising the essential diversity of the situations of underdevelopment. Such extended theories, on the contrary, have sought to homogenise the diverse situations of underdevelopment. Even before their extensions into development studies, such theories rarely came to terms with the fact of plurality in the situations of their origin. In fact both William James and John Dewey, to some extent, wrote several critiques of Western philosophical theories trying to treat social reality as 'a block universe'.[18]

But apart from that, the cultivating of sensitivity to plurality never became an intellectually respectable exercise in the social sciences. At best it remained a negative tool in the hands of critics, who used it to shoot down someone else's shiny theory when it ignored the fact of variety and plurality.

Semantically and conceptually, there is a difference between variety, on the one hand, and plurality, on the other. The dictionary meaning of 'variety' is 'The fact, quality or condition of being varied; diversity of nature or character; absence of monotony, sameness, or uniformity.'[19] Plurality, and the philosophical doctrine derived from it, namely, pluralism, imply that 'the knowable world is made up of a plurality of interacting things.'[20]

Thus in the context of development studies, one could say that variety refers to the diversity of situations and plurality, as a principle, to the presence of lasting patterns of diversity in the world of development.

In order to engage in theory construction in development, we need to recognise the presence of a variety of social and historical antecedents leading to differing processes of development and conditions of underdevelopment, some of which, over a period of time may settle into lasting patterns. Simultaneously, by the same logic we need to recognise the internal variety within each pattern, producing its own internal plurality of crystallised subpatterns.

Phasing or weaving the variety and plurality dimensions into our theoretical thinking in development studies is not going to be easy. But we cannot live without it either, because the baffling variety of development processes and the plurality of their settled patterns, as we have argued throughout this book, register themselves so unmistakably for our scholarly attention.

For a long time we have neglected the variety and plurality of our development experiences because of the homogenistic constraints imposed by our earlier rounds of theory construction. And given the background of social science theory, which we borrowed earlier without many qualifications, and also the genuine difficulty of coming to terms with the fact of variety and plurality, our efforts at development theory construction will be a massive undertaking. We shall have to build, incrementally, and continually test, our theory constructions in development studies. For this we need to go back, again and again, to the actuality and diversity of development processes at a level, preferably grassroots, at which we can get an increasingly deeper understanding of them. That means that we can initially come up with theoretical explanations of only specific and limited areas of research. These will then have to be pieced together in an ever-widening area of explanations and theory constructions.

Such a theory of theories can be built only gradually, ever facing the challenges of development particularism, step by step, in contrast to the old parlour game of replacing one unserious theory by another.

This will also mean that we shall periodically pass through a phase when we do not trust the old theories of development but at the same time do not have the new ones to replace them. Such a situation of theoretical unsettlement is unavoidable. But that is the price development theory will have to pay for rediscovering the non-Western world and becoming an integral part of its development effort.

Notes and References

Preface

1. A.H. Somjee, *Parallels and Actuals of Political Development* (London: Macmillan, 1986).
2. Gunnar Myrdal, *An Approach to the Asian Drama: Methodological and Theoretical* (New York: Vintage Books, 1970) p. 26.
3. Albert O. Hirschman, *Essays in Trespassing: Economics to Politics and Beyond* (London: Cambridge University Press, 1981) p. v.
4. Karl Popper, in his earlier writings, especially meant for historians and social scientists, had argued his case against inductive knowledge as follows: 'I do not believe that we ever make inductive generalizations in the same sense we start with observations and try to derive our theories from them.' For him, 'inductive knowledge' is an 'optical illusion'. 'At no stage of scientific development do we begin without something in the nature of a theory such as hypothesis, or a prejudice, or a problem – often a technical one – which in some way *guides* our observations.' After taking such a position Popper became more concerned with how theories are tested rather than arrived at. In his words: 'It is irrelevant from the point of view of science whether we have obtained our theories by jumping to unwarranted conclusions or merely by stumbling over them (that is "intuition"), or else by some inductive procedure. The question "How did you *find* your theory?" relates, as it were, to an entirely private matter, as opposed to the question, "How did you *test* your theory?" which alone is scientifically relevant.' See in this connection Karl R. Popper, *The Poverty of Historicism* (New York: Harper Torchbooks, 1964) pp. 134–5. Unlike the above position, where Popper becomes at times ambivalent towards inductive knowledge, his subsequent writings take a firmer stance against such knowledge. Popper, nevertheless, did not go deep enough into the question of what in fact happens within the process of enquiry when an initial hypothesis breaks down and when the available data are there for us to explore what else they can sustain by way of reconstructed hypothesis. The idea here is to accord as much importance to the existential situations, experiences and so on, as we accord to our conceptual tools. Also see in this connection Karl R. Popper, *Objective Knowledge: An Evolutionary Approach* (Oxford: Clarendon press, 1973) pp. 85–105, David Stove, *Popper and After* (Oxford: Pergamon Press, 1982) pp. 50–2, and D.C. Stove, *The Rationality of Induction* (Oxford: Clarendon Press, 1986).
5. See in this connection Max Weber, *The Theory of Social and Economic Organization*, edited by Talcott Parsons (London: Collier-Macmillan, 1965) pp. 87–8, and George A. Theodorson and Achilles G.

174

Theodorson, *A Modern Dictionary of Sociology* (London: Methuen, 1970) p. 460.

6. See Edwin Ardener, 'Belief and the Problem of Women', in Shirley Ardener (ed.), *Perceiving Women* (London: J.M. Dent, 1975) pp. 1–19.

7. Joseph A. Schumpeter, *The Theory of Economic Development* (Cambridge, Mass.: Harvard University Press, 1934) pp. 3–5.

8. See in this connection A.H. Somjee and Geeta Somjee, 'Cooperative Dairying and the Profiles of Social Change in India', in *Economic Development and Cultural Change*, 1978. Also William Rowe, 'The New Cauhans: A Caste Mobility Movement in Northern India', in James Silverberg (ed.), *Social Mobility in the Caste System in India* (The Hague: Mouton, 1968), and F.G. Bailey, *Caste, Tribe and Nation* (Manchester: Manchester University Press, 1960).

9. See in this connection Geeta Somjee and A.H. Somjee, *Reaching Out to the Poor* (London: Macmillan, 1989).

Chapter 1

1. Quoted by Paul Streeten, *Development Perspectives* (London: Macmillan, 1981) p. 97.

2. Ibid., p. 104.

3. Ibid., p. 110.

4. A.F.K. Organski, *The Stages of Political Development* (New York: Alfred A. Knopf, 1965).

5. Gabriel A. Almond and James Coleman (eds), *The Politics of the Developing Areas* (Princeton, NJ: Princeton University Press, 1960) p. 4.

6. Gabriel A. Almond and Sidney Verba, *The Civic Culture: Political Attitudes and Democracy in Five Nations* (Princeton, NJ: Princeton University Press, 1963).

7. Lucian W. Pye, *Aspects of Political Development* (Boston, Mass.: Little, Brown, 1966).

8. See in this connection Alexis de Tocqeville, *Democracy in America* (New York: Vintage Books, 1945).

9. See in this connection Wilbert E. Moore, *Social Change* (Engelwood Cliffs, NJ: Prentice-Hall, 1963) p. 30.

10. Max Weber, *General Economic History* (Glencoe, Illinois: Free Press, 1950) pp. 27–111 *passim* and 275–313.

11. Marx and Engels, *Manifesto of the Communist Party*, in Robert Tucker (ed.), *The Marx-Engels Reader*, 2nd edn. (New York: W.W. Norton, 1978) pp. 469–500.

12. Max Weber, 'The Psychology of World Religions', in H.H. Gerth and C. Wright Mills (eds), *From Max Weber* (Oxford: Oxford University Press, 1948) p. 268.

13. In his foreword to Max Weber, *The Protestant Ethic and the Spirit of*

Capitalism (New York: Charles Scribner's Sons, 1958) p. 2.

14. Max Weber, *General Economic History*, pp. 27–111 *passim* and 275–313.

15. Max Weber, *The Theory of Social and Economic Organization*, pp. 342–92.

16. From Talcott Parsons's introduction to Max Weber, *The Theory of Social and Economic Organization*, p. 31.

17. Erma Edelman and Cynthia Morris, *Society, Politics and Economic Development* (Baltimore: Johns Hopkins University Press, 1967) p. vii.

18. Ibid., p. 4.

19. Everett Hagen, *On the Theory of Social Change: How Economic Growth Begins* (Homewood, Illinois: The Dorsey Press, 1962) p. vii.

20. Ibid., p. x.

21. *Passim* p. 3.

22. Ibid., p. 4.

23. Ibid., p. 5.

24. Michael Lipton, 'Interdisciplinary Studies in Less Developed Countries', in *The Journal of Development Studies*, vol. VII, 1970, pp. 5–18.

25. Barrington Moore Jr, *Social Origins of Dictatorship and Democracy: The Lord and the Peasant in the Making of the Modern World* (Boston, Mass.: Beacon Press, 1966).

26. S.M. Lipset, *The Political Man: The Social Bases of Politics* (New York: Anchor Books, 1963).

27. Phillips Cutright, 'National Political Development: Social and Economic Correlates', in Nelson W. Polsby et al. (eds), *Politics and Social Life* (Boston: Houghton Mifflin, 1963).

28. See in this connection Lee Siegelman, *Modernization and Political System: A Critique and Preliminary Analysis* (Beverly Hills, California: Sage Foundation, 1971).

29. Neil J. Smelser and Samuel Martin Lipset (eds), *Social Structure and Mobility in Economic Development* (Chicago: Aldine, 1966).

30. Joseph A. Schumpeter, *The Theory of Economic Development*, p. 3.

31. Ibid., pp. 4–5.

32. Ibid., p. 58. Italics in the text.

33. Gunnar Myrdal, *An Approach to the Asian Drama: Methodological and Theoretical*, p. 26.

34. In 1973, I sent Gunnar Myrdal a copy of my longitudinal study of a rural community in western India entitled *Democracy and Political Change in Village India: A Case-Study* (New Delhi: Orient Longman, 1972), and in reply he wrote: 'It is just that type of studies which are very much needed.'

35. See in this connection an excellent paper entitled 'Gunnar Myrdal' by Paul Streeten, in *Development Perspectives* (London: Macmillan, 1981) pp. 418–31.

36. Ibid., p. 421.

37. Quoted by Paul Streeten, ibid., pp. 422–3.

38. Albert O. Hirschman, *Essays in Trespassing: Economics to Politics and Beyond.*, p. v.

39. Ibid., p. 5.
40. Ibid., p. 37.
41. Albert O. Hirschman, *The Passion and the Interests: Political Arguments For Capitalism before its Triumph* (Princeton, NJ: Princeton University Press, 1977) p. 3.
42. Albert O. Hirschman, *Getting Ahead Collectively: Grassroots Experiences in Latin America* (New York: Pergamon Press, 1984).
43. Bert Hoselitz, *Sociological Aspects of Economic Growth* (Glencoe, Illinois: Free Press, 1960) p. 3.
44. Ibid., p. 5.
45. Ibid., pp. 23–4.
46. 'Interdisciplinary Studies in Less Developed Countries', by Michael Lipton, in *The Journal of Development Studies*, vol. VII, 1970, pp. 5–18.
47. Amartya Sen, *Resources, Values and Development* (Oxford: Basil Blackwell, 1984).
48. A.H. Somjee, *Parallels and Actuals of Political Development*.
49. Samuel P. Huntington and Joan Nelson, *No Easy Choice: Political Participation in Developing Countries* (Cambridge, Mass.: Harvard University Press, 1976).

Chapter 2

1. Bert Hoselitz, *Sociological Aspects of Economic Growth*, p. 28, my italics.
2. Fernand Braudel, *Capitalism and Material Life: 1400–1800* (New York: Harper & Row, 1967) p. 445.
3. Max Weber, *The Protestant Ethic and the Spirit of Capitalism*.
4. Bert Hoselitz, *Sociological Aspects of Economic Growth*, p. 107.
5. Max Weber, *The Protestant Ethic and the Spirit of Capitalism*, pp. 47–78.
6. Max Weber, *General Economic History*, pp. 120–313.
7. Ibid., p. 354.
8. R.H. Tawney, *Religion and the Rise of Capitalism* (New York: Harcourt, Brace and Co., 1926) p. ix.
9. Ibid., p. 8.
10. S.N. Eisenstadt (ed.), *The Protestant Ethic and Modernization: A Comparative View* (New York: Basic Books, 1968) p. 6.
11. In his foreword to Max Weber, *The Protestant Ethic and the Spirit of Capitalism*, p. 2.
12. S.N. Eisenstadt, *The Protestant Ethic and Modernization*, p. 8.
13. Ibid. pp. 10–60
14. Karl de Schweinitz Jr, *Industrialization and Democracy: Economic Necessities and Political Possibilities* (London: Collier-Macmillan, 1964) p. 3.
15. Ibid., pp. 10–11.

16. Barrington Moore Jr, *Social Origins of Dictatorship and Democracy: The Lord and the Peasant in the Making of the Modern World.*

17. See in this connection *Poverty and Un-British Rule in India* (London: 1901), and *India and the Currency Question: A Pamphlet* (London: 1898).

18. Fernando Henrique Cordoso and Enzo Faletto, *Dependency and Development in Latin America* (Berkeley, California: California University Press, 1979), p. viii.

19. Paul A. Baran, *The Political Economy of Growth* (New York: Modern Reader Paperbacks, 1957) p. 122.

20. Andre Gunder Frank, 'The Development of Underdevelopment', in James D. Cockcroft et al. (eds), *Dependence and Underdevelopment* (New York: Anchor Books, 1972) pp. 3–19.

21. Cordoso and Faletto, *Dependency and Development in Latin America*, p. ix.

22. Ibid., p. xv.

23. Ibid., p. xvi.

24. Ibid., p. 173.

25. Magnus Blomstorm and Bjorn Hettne, *Development Theory in Transition* (London: Zed Books, 1984) pp. 70–84 *passim.*

26. Ibid., p. 90.

27. Ibid., p. 107.

28. Guillermo A. O'Donnell, 'Corporatism and the Question of the State' in James M. Malloy (ed.), *Authoritarianism and Corporatism in Latin America* (Pittsburgh: University of Pittsburgh Press, 1977).

29. See in this connection A.H. Somjee, *Political Society in Developing Countries* (London: Macmillan, 1984) pp. 169–80.

30. See in this connection Howard Wiarda, *Corporatism and National Development in Latin America* (Boulder, Colorado: West View Press, 1981).

31. Guillermo O'Donnell, 'Corporatism and the Question of the State', in *Authoritarianism and Corporatism in Latin America* (Pittsburgh: University of Pittsburgh Press, 1977) pp. 52–77 *passim.* Also see Juan J. Linz, 'The Future of Authoritarian Situations on the Institutionalization of An Authoritarian State: The Case of Brazil', in Alfred Stepan (ed.), *Authoritarian Brazil: Origins, Policies, Future* (New Haven, Conn.: Yale University Press, 1973).

32. Chie Nakane, *Japanese Society* (Berkeley, California: California University Press, 1970) p. viii.

33. Ibid., p. ix.

34. Ibid., p. 6.

35. Ibid., p. 15.

36. Michio Morishima, *Why has Japan 'Succeeded'? Western Technology and Japanese Ethos* (Cambridge: Cambridge University Press, 1982) p. viii.

37. Ibid., p. 2.

38. Ibid., p. 19.

39. Robert Bellah in his 'Reflections on the Protestant Ethic Analogy in Asia' has raised the question of 'this worldly asceticism', as preached

by some of the religious sects in Asia, helping their followers to become effective savers and builders of capital. Milton Singer, also quoted by Bellah in that article, argued that 'the ethic austerity', as opposed to materialist values, may have helped some of those sects in their economic advancement. But the example of Japan seems to be different. Her economic growth, her social organisation, traditional values, habits of work, group effort, education, and constant learning of new skills, all these together present a very different picture. See Robert Bellah in S.N. Eisenstadt (ed.), *The Protestant Ethic and Modernization*, pp. 243–4.

40. See in this connection 'Multilayered Political Societies and Conceptual Inadequacy', in A.H. Somjee, *Parallels and Actuals of Political Development*, pp. 60–101. Also see in this connection, Yogerk Atal, 'The Call for Indigenization', in *International Social Science Journal*, Vol.XXXIII, no.1, 1981.
41. A.W. Burks, *Japan: Profile of a Post-Industrial Power* (Boulder, Colorado: West View Press, 1981) p. 39.
42. Solomon B. Levine and Hishashi Kawada, *Human Resources in Japanese Industrial Development* (Princeton, NJ: Princeton University Press, 1980) p. 5.
43. Ronald Dore, *Taking Japan Seriously: A Confucian Perspective on Leading Economic Issues* (Stanford: Stanford University Press, 1987) p. viii.
44. See in this connection Ronald Dore, *City Life in Japan: A Study of Tokyo Ward* (London: Routledge and Kegan Paul, 1958) p. 378, and Ezra Vogel, *Japan as Number One: Lessons For America* (Cambridge, Mass.: Harvard University Press, 1979).
45. Kinhide Mushakoji, *Global Issues and Interparadigmatic Dialogue: Essays on Multipolar Politics* (Torino: Albert Meynier, 1988) p. 3.
46. Gilbert Rozman (ed.), *The Modernization of China* (London: Collier-Macmillan, 1981) p. 14.
47. See in this connection a highly perceptive paper entitled 'Sinological Shadows: The State of Modern China Studies in the US' by Thomas A. Metzger and Ramon H. Myers, in Amy Auerbacher Wilson, Sidney Leonard Greenblatt, and Richard W. Wilson (eds), *Methodological Issues in Chinese Studies* (New York: Prager Special Studies, 1983) pp. 14–50.
48. Gilbert Rozman (ed.), *The Modernization of China*, p. 494.
49. Lin Wei and Arnold Chao (eds), *China's Economic Reforms* (Philadelphia: University of Pennsylvania Press, 1982) p. ix.
50. Ibid. pp. 115–187.
51. Yu Guangyan, 'Lenin's Expositions on State Capitalism Under Proletarian Dictatorship and My Related Observations', in *Selected Studies in Marxism*, edited by Institute of Marxism–Leninism and Mao Zedong Thought, Chinese Academy of Social Sciences, Beijing, Numbers 1–6, 1985, pp. 18–19.
52. Su Shaozhi, 'Develop Marxism Under Contemporary Conditions', in *Selected Studies on Marxism* (Beijing, 1984) p. 34.
53. See in this connection A.H. Somjee, *Parallels and Actuals of Political Development*, pp. 89–90.

54. Ping-ti Ho and Tang Tsou (eds), *China's Heritage and Communist Political System* (Chicago: Chicago University Press, 1968). Also see Thomas A. Metzger, *Escape From Predicament: Neo-Confucianism and China's Evolving Political Culture* (New York: Columbia University Press, 1977).
55. Pranab Bardhan, *The Political Economy of Development in India* (Oxford: Basil Blackwell, 1984) p. 10.
56. T. Roychaudhuri, quoted in Jagdish Bhagwati and Padma Desai, *India: Planning For Industrialization* (London: Oxford University Press, 1970) p. 14. Italics in the text.
57. Kenneth L. Gillon, *Ahmedabad: A Study in the Indian Urban History* (Berkeley, California: California University Press, 1968).
58. Pranab Bardhan, *The Political Economy of Development in India*, pp. 1–2.
59. Ibid. pp. 4–5
60. Amartya Sen, *Poverty and Famines: An Essay on Entitlement and Deprivation* (Oxford: Clarendon Press, 1982) pp. vii–viii.
61. See in this connection Geeta Somjee and A.H. Somjee, *Reaching Out to the Poor*.
62. Pranab Bardhan, *Land, Labour, and Rural Poverty: Essays in Development Economics* (New York: Columbia University Press, 1984) p. 3.
63. Amaraty Sen, *Employment, Technology and Development* (Oxford: Clarendon Press, 1975) p. 115. Also see Sanjay Lall and Frances Stewart (eds), *Theory and Reality in Development* (London: Macmillan, 1986) and V.V. Bhatt, *Development Perspectives: Problem, Strategy, and Policies* (Oxford: Pergamon Press, 1980) p. xiii.
64. Philip Mason, 'Unity and Diversity: An Introductory Review', in Philip Mason, (ed.), *India and Ceylon: Unity and Diversity* (London: Oxford University Press, 1967) p. 28.
65. Dr Altekar, quoted by Jayaprakash Narayan in *A Plea For Reconstruction Of Indian Polity* (Kashi: Akhil Bharat Sarva Seva Sangh Prakashan, no date) p. 28.
66. Ibid., p. 31.
67. Balwantray Mehta Committee Report, 1957.
68. A.H. Somjee, *Democracy and Political Change in Village India*.
69. Geeta Somjee and A.H. Somjee, *Reaching Out to the Poor*, 1989.
70. A.H. Somjee, *Parallels and Actuals of Political Development*, 1986.

Chapter 3

1. J.M. Letiche, 'Adam Smith and David Ricardo on Economic Growth', in Bert Hoselitz (ed.), *Theories of Economic Growth* (London: Collier-Macmillan, 1960) pp. 65–70 *passim*.
2. Ibid., p. 76.
3. Joseph J. Spengler, 'John Stuart Mill on Economic Development', in Bert Hoselitz (ed.), *Theories of Economic Growth*, p. 117.

4. Ragnar Nurske, *Problems of Capital Formation in Underdeveloped Countries*, 10th impression (New York: Oxford University Press, 1966) p. 1.
5. Robert Heilbronner, *The Worldly Philosophers* (New York: Simon and Schuster, 1972) p. 14.
6. M.N. Srinivas, *Social Change in Modern India* (Berkeley, California: California University Press, 1968) pp. 114–16.
7. See in this connection 'An Emerging Political Society', in A.H. Somjee, *Democratic Process in A Developing Society* (London: Macmillan, 1979) pp. 125–45.
8. Figures quoted by *India News* (courtesy *The Hindu*), July 1989.
9. See for the details of this A.H. Somjee and Geeta Somjee 'Cooperative Dairying and the Profiles of Social Change in India', in *Economic Development and Cultural Change*, Chicago 1978.
10. For the details of the establishment of Amul, see Geeta Somjee and A.H. Somjee, *Reaching Out to the Poor*.
11. See in this connection John Empson, 'Uneasy Flow of Third World Milk', in *Financial Times*, 16 February 1989.
12. The dilemma and the agony of Chaudhury women in switching from the *mehsani* to the cross-bred cows is recorded in Geeta Somjee's *Narrowing the Gender Gap* (London: Macmillan, 1989) pp. 107–11.
13. See for the details of méga milk economies of rural Mehsana, Geeta Somjee and A.H. Somjee, *Reaching Out To The Poor*.
14. See for a detailed comparison of the performance in dairying of tribal villages with or without the Chaudhury population, ibid., pp. 125–32.
15. See for details of this effort, ibid., pp. 72–81.
16. See for details of this, ibid., pp. 81–104 and 136–47. Also see A.H. Somjee, *Political Capacity in Developing Societies* (London: Macmillan, 1982).
17. See for details of this process a longitudinal study by A.H. Somjee, *Democracy and Political Change in Village India: A Case-Study*.
18. 'Normative-Pragmatic Considerations in Political Involvement', in A.H. Somjee, *Political Society in Developing Countries*, pp. 78–124.

Chapter 4

1. See in this connection Chapter 1, note 4.
2. For criticism of Soviet studies from this point of view, see Jerry F. Hough, *The Soviet Union and Social Science Theory* (Cambridge, Mass.: Harvard University Press, 1977).
3. Ibid., p. 14.
4. A.H. Somjee, *Political Capacity in Developing Societies*, pp. 32–59.
5. See in this connection A.H. Somjee, *Democracy and Political Change in Village India: A Case-Study*.
6. A.H. Somjee, 'Caste and the Decline of Political Homogeneity',

in *American Political Science Review*, September 1973.

7.   A.H. Somjee, *Political Capacity in Developing Societies*, pp. 41–53.
8.   A.H. Somjee, *Democratic Process in A Developing Society*.
9.   M.N. Srinivas has argued that the horizontal consolidation of castes occurred as a result of the law and order provided by British rule in India. See in this connection his *Caste in Modern India And Other Essays* (Bombay: Asia Publishing House, 1962) pp. 70–6.
10. Max Weber, 'Class, Status and Party', in H.H. Gerth and C. Wright Mills (eds),*From Max Weber: Essays in Sociology* (London: Kegan Paul, Trench, Trubner & Co, 1947) pp. 188–9.
11. Geeta Somjee and A.H. Somjee, *Reaching Out To The Poor*, pp. 136–47.
12. A.H. Somjee and Geeta Somjee, 'Cooperative Dairying and the Profiles of Social Change in India', in *Economic Development and Cultural Change*.
13. William Rowe, 'The New Cauhans: A Caste Mobility Movement in Northern India'.
14. F.G. Bailey, *Caste, Tribe and Nation* (Manchester: Manchester University Press, 1960).
15. See for details of this process A.H. Somjee, *Political Society in Developing Countries*.
16. Geeta Somjee and A.H. Somjee, *Reaching Out To The Poor*.
17. Max Weber, *The Protestant Ethic and the Spirit of Capitalism*.
18. A.H. Somjee, *The Political Theory of John Dewey* (New York: Teachers' College Columbia University Press, 1968).
19. *The Oxford English Dictionary*, 2nd edn (Oxford: Clarendon Press, 1964) vol. xix, p. 446.
20. Ibid., vol. xi, p. 1089.

Index